ANTHROPOLOGICAL PAPERS

MUSEUM OF ANTHROPOLOGY, UNIVERSITY OF MICHIGAN

No. 11

Late Pleistocene Geochronology and the Paleo-Indian Penetration into the Lower Michigan Peninsula

by

RONALD J. MASON

ANN ARBOR
UNIVERSITY OF MICHIGAN, 1958

ISBN (print): 978-1-949098-32-7
ISBN (ebook): 978-1-951519-56-8

Browse all of our books at
sites.lsa.umich.edu/archaeology-books.

Order our books from the University of Michigan
Press at www.press.umich.edu.

For permissions, questions, or manuscript queries,
contact Museum publications by email at umma-
pubs@umich.edu or visit the Museum website at
lsa.umich.edu/ummaa.

CONTENTS

	Page
Introduction	1
Distributional Data	3
Description of Fluted Points	7
Manufacture and Shaping of the Blade	7
Fluting Techniques	12
Length of Fluting and Length of Fluting Scar — A Distinction	14
Blade Configuration	15
Review of Geochronology of Lower Peninsula of Michigan and of Adjacent Great Lakes Basins	17
Cary Subage	17
Mankato Subage	21
Two Creeks Interstadial	23
Valders Subage	23
Post-Valders Maximum	25
Xerothermic and Post-Xerothermic	26
Suggested Correlations of Fluted Point Loci and Late Pleistocene Events	30
Berrien and Cass Counties	30
Washtenaw County	32
Ottawa, Allegan, and Van Buren Counties	33
Newaygo and Mecosta Counties	34
Bay and Wayne Counties	34
Other Localities	35
Remarks	35
Comparisons and Discussion	37
Comparative Material from Wisconsin	37
Comparative Material from Ontario	39
St. Louis Area of Missouri and Illinois	39
Ohio-Pennsylvania Area	40
Eastern Pennsylvania, New Jersey, Delaware, and Virginia	41
New England Fluted Points	42
Summary and Conclusions	44
Literature Cited	46

ILLUSTRATIONS

PLATES

(Plates I - IX follow page 48)

PLATE

I. Fluted points from Michigan: Saginaw, Washtenaw, Lapeer, and county unknown.

II. Fluted points from Michigan: Lapeer, Washtenaw, and county unknown.

III. Fluted points from Michigan: Washtenaw, Hillsdale, and Lapeer counties.

IV. Fluted points from Michigan: Ionia, Washtenaw, and county unknown.

V. Fluted blade from Michigan: Washtenaw County.

VI. Fluted points from Michigan: Washtenaw County.

VII. Fluted-point fragments from Michigan: Berrien and Lapeer counties.

VIII. Fluted points from Michigan: Allegan and Berrien counties.

IX. Fluted points from Michigan: St. Joseph, Berrien, and Van Buren counties.

FIGURES IN THE TEXT

FIGURE		Page
1.	Shapes of fluted points from Cass County	6
2.	Two fluting techniques suggested by an examination of fluted points from Michigan	13
3.	Blade configuration of two fluted points from Waukesha County, Wisconsin	38

MAPS

MAP		
1.	Distribution of fluted blades in Michigan.	4
2.	Major Late Pleistocene morainic systems of the Lake Michigan lobe of the Wisconsin ice sheet.	18
3.	Michigan during the Mankato Maximum	20
4.	Michigan during the Valders Maximum	22
5.	Michigan during the Algonquin Lake stage	24

INTRODUCTION

A widely recognized but as yet poorly understood Paleo-Indian cultural horizon comparable to High Plains fluted-blade industries has been thought by archaeologists in recent years to initiate the prehistory of man in most of the eastern United States and immediately adjacent areas of Canada. This seemingly early infiltration of big-game hunting peoples has been inferred from increasing finds of scattered fluted points and from a few assemblages of such points and other kinds of specialized tools. The list of sites east of the Mississippi River having such assemblages is short, but it has grown rapidly in recent years.

Eastern fluted points (or blades, as they are sometimes called) exhibit great range in size, blade and basal configuration, extent of fluting, technique of manufacture, and type of material. At the time of this writing no clear faunal associations are known for these interesting artifacts and estimates of their age and specific cultural relationships are based on typological and, to a much lesser extent, geochronological grounds. Probably the paramount need at present, lacking good stratigraphic data and associated fossils, is more information on the distribution and typology of eastern fluted projectile points. This examination of applicable material from Michigan will, it is hoped, fill, at least partially, one of the many gaps in our knowledge of Early Man in the Northeast. Additionally, this study was undertaken to determine if the combined distributional, typological, and geochronological data would support or refute a recent provocative estimate of the probable bottom date for the earliest influx of Paleo-Indians into Michigan, the suggested time level being about 12,500 years ago (Greenman, Griffin, and Spaulding, 1956).

The distributional study is based on 115 Michigan fluted points for which there is reliable information at least as to general provenience. Find localities of some of these are precisely known and have been employed in attempting correlations with geochronological data. It is freely admitted that surface finds may be inferior to excavated material when geochronological reckoning is proposed, especially if emphasis is placed upon the provenience of only a few specimens. Since some provenience information is now available for 115 specimens, it is judged that an examination of this distribution will have value as a general clue to the beginning and end dates of the Paleo-Indian occupation of the state. I assume that most, if not all, of the artifacts were discovered where originally deposited, and that any subsequent disturbance has been no more than local.

Of the total sample, twenty specimens are in the collections of the Museum of Anthropology of the University of Michigan, where this study was made. Information on other finds has been gleaned from records, photographs, and correspondence in the Museum files. George R. Fox of Dowagiac, Amos R. Green of Eau Claire, Robert A. Hard of Fenton, and Harold W. Moll of Midland, members of the Michigan Archaeological Society, supplied invaluable information. I am also indebted to Leslie Archer, Paul Armintrout, Eldon S. Cornelius, R. G. Curtis, George Franklin, Harvey Franz, Charles Garlanger, Joel Gillette, Ed Hyde, Harold J. King, Mrs. Donald Messer, Guy Nelson, Leon W. North, Karl G. Parchert, Sylvester Poltorak, A. L. Spooner, and Mrs. Ida Yaggie, all of whom helped directly or indirectly in the gathering of information. Some of these individuals supplied data and, in some instances, actual specimens were furnished through the kind offices of Messrs. Fox, Green, Hard, and Moll.

A few of the find loci were discussed in March, 1957, with George I. Quimby, of the Chicago Natural History Museum, who has been making an independent study of some of the fluted-point localities in western Michigan and eastern Wisconsin in order to correlate them with glacial lake stages in the Lake Michigan basin. In the few areas in which our investigations overlapped, our independent conclusions were largely compatible at the time of our discussion. I also wish to acknowledge the stimulating encouragement and constructive criticisms of Dr. James B. Griffin, Dr. Emerson F. Greenman, and Dr. Albert C. Spaulding of the Museum of Anthropology, University of Michigan, and Dr. James H. Zumberge, glaciologist and Pleistocene geologist at the University of Michigan, who helped guide me over the rocky road of Late Wisconsin geochronology. Errors of omission or commission are, of course, my responsibility entirely.

Finally, my thanks are due Makoto Kowta, formerly of the Museum of Anthropology, University of Michigan, now at the University of California, who kindly supplied the photographs, and to Phyllis A. S. Anderson, of the Museum of Anthropology, University of Michigan, who read proof.

DISTRIBUTIONAL DATA

The gross geographic distribution of the 115 fluted blades from Michigan is presented by counties in Table I and, with more specificity, in Map 1. Where greater detail is available, it is given in the ensuing sections relating particular loci to physical features of Late Wisconsin age.

Initially, the following observations may be made. All fluted points known to have been discovered in Michigan are from the southern half of the Lower Peninsula; none have been reported from the Upper Peninsula. Approximately 70 per cent of the specimens are from the extreme southern part of the Lower Peninsula, and 55 per cent are restricted to the southwestern corner, almost all of these coming from counties adjacent to the Indiana state line. There is a possibility that the discovery of such a large number of points from this area is a result of more intensive surface collecting in that part of the state. It should be pointed out, however, that this is the region which was first opened up to human occupancy at the time levels with which we are concerned.

The most northerly penetration of the fluted-blade makers known to date is manifested by the finds to the east in Bay County, on Saginaw Bay, and those to the west in Midland County. A little farther to the south, in central Michigan, the most northerly finds of fluted points are from Mecosta County and, closer to Lake Michigan, from Newaygo

TABLE I

Distribution of Fluted Blades in Michigan by Counties

Three additional specimens from Michigan cannot be localized. This raises the total to 118.

County	No.	County	No.
Allegan	2	Mecosta	5
Bay	2	Midland	6
Berrien	29	Newaygo	3
Cass	26	Ottawa	1
Genesee	3	Saginaw	5
Hillsdale	2	St. Joseph	2
Ingham	1	Tuscola	1
Ionia	2	Van Buren	2
Kent	2	Washtenaw	12
Lapeer	6	Wayne	2
Livingston	1	Total	115

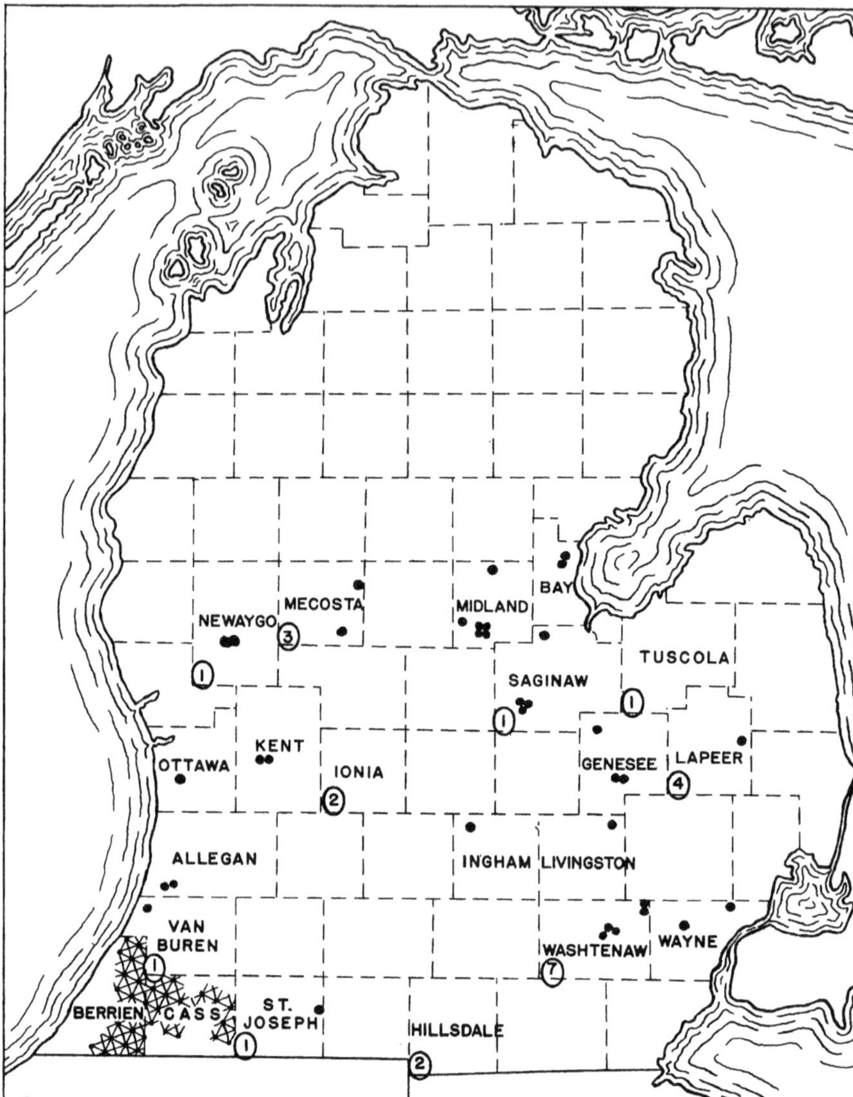

Map 1. Distribution of fluted blades in Michigan. Each dot represents the locus of a particular find. The hatched area in Berrien and Cass counties indicates the high incidence of finds in that area. Figures encircled represent the number of other fluted points found in each county for which specific provenience data is lacking.

County. Fluted points, then, have a scattered distribution in the southern half of the Lower Peninsula, but a few specific areas exhibit some clusterings.

To give additional distributional data here would duplicate information to be presented later, when the archaeological and geological material are considered together in those cases for which correlations may be suggested. Before this is done these artifacts are described and the geochronology of lower Michigan that is pertinent to an understanding of where in time these fluted blades belong is examined briefly.

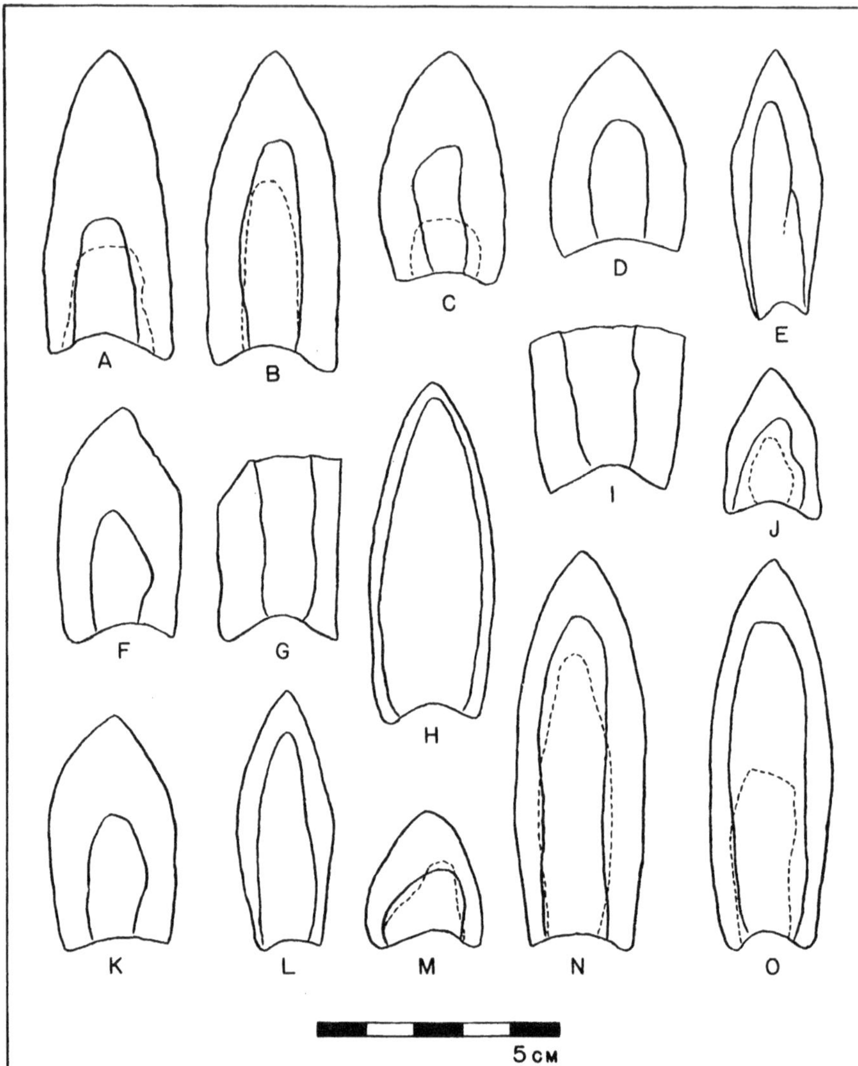

Fig. 1. Shapes of Fluted Points from Cass County (after drawings supplied by George R. Fox).

A, J, and M, Wayne Township; B, Volinia; C, Jefferson; D and F, North Porter; E and I, Newberg; G, LaGrange; H, Silver Creek; K, L, and N, Unknown Township; and O, Pokagon.

DESCRIPTION OF FLUTED POINTS

Specific measurements of these specimens for which such data is available are given in Tables II through V, and a representative sample is illustrated (see plates). Outline drawings of additional fluted points from Cass County are given in Figure 1, and descriptions of broken and fragmentary specimens, where tied in with geochronological data, are included in those parts of the text dealing with the loci involved. In the general description and analysis of the Michigan material, some statements apply equally to comparable series of fluted points from other parts of the northeastern United States and adjacent sections of Canada.

Manufacture and Shaping of the Blade

From the few examples of unfinished fluted points and a study of longitudinal and transverse cross sections of finished specimens, it seems that Michigan fluted blades were based on generally large ovoid flakes struck from nonprismatic cores, the bulbar ends of such flakes frequently defining the site of the tip end of the projectile point to be manufactured. This observation applies to many fluted points from the East, particularly from Pennsylvania, New Jersey, Delaware, Virginia, and eastern Ohio, which I have personally examined. Whether or not it may also apply to High Plains industries must be determined by workers more directly familiar with that material. On some Michigan specimens (Plate III, C) there are a few areas which have been identified as original flake-facet retentions; that is, part or parts of a flake facet of the original flake upon which the projectile point was based were not completely obliterated by blade-shaping and fluting processes, and thus were retained on the finished artifact. This interesting feature, although relatively rare, has also been observed on specimens from the other regions of the East mentioned above. The flake facet can be identified readily by such criteria as conformity of the suspected facet with the over-all cross-sectional configuration of the blade, nonconformity with the blade's flaking pattern, and differential patination or other weathering characteristics.

Michigan fluted blades, while sometimes exhibiting fine flint control, are certainly inferior to the workmanship seen on Folsom blades and are, as many workers have recognized for other eastern assemblages, both formally and technologically more closely related to Clovis. Variations of the Michigan fluted blades in size and shape are less restricted than is the case with Folsom, and a generally poorer control of the flint is always evident. The Michigan series illustrates a high incidence of hinge fractures terminating fluting scars. Pronounced rippling,

TABLE II

Measurements (in Millimeters) of Michigan Fluted Points

Specimens are those illustrated on plates. The ones on Plate VIII, A and B, are from the Paul Armintrout Collection; on Plate VIII, C, and IX, B, from the Amos R. Green Collection; and IX, C, is from the Guy Nelson Collection. The rest are in the collections of the Museum of Anthropology, University of Michigan.

Plate	No.	Material	Blade Length	Max. Width	Max. Thick-ness	Extent Lateral Grind-ing	Basal Width	Basal Depth	Basal Grind-ing	Fluting Scar Length		Multiple Channel Scars	Provenience (County)
										Obverse	Reverse		
I	A	Chert	42.5	20.5	6.0	23.0	16.5	2.0	X	18.0H	. . .	X	Saginaw
I	B	Flint	40.0	22.0	4.5	22.0	22.0	3.5	X	32.0	24.0	. . .	Unknown
I	C	Chert	78.0	23.0	7.0	22.0	21.0*	3.0*	X	47.0	31.0	. . .	Lapeer
I	D	Chert	69.0	24.0	7.0	25.0	18.0*	3.0*	X	57.0	50.0	X	Washtenaw (Salem)
II	A	Chert	53.0*	23.5	5.5	20.0	20.0	4.0	X	35.0H	24.0H	?	Lapeer
II	B	Chert	52.0	18.0	5.5	30.0	14.5	2.5	X	24.0H	9.0H	X	Lapeer
II	C	Chert	60.0	25.0	8.0	27.5	25.0	3.5	X	25.0H	25.0H	?	Unknown
II	D	Flint	58.0	22.0	7.5	0	22.0	4.5	X	13.0H	12.5H	. . .	Washtenaw
III	A	Flint	62.0	27.0	8.0	34.0	24.5	5.5	X	43.0H	29.0H	. . .	Washtenaw
III	B	Chert	50.0	19.5	6.0	22.0	16.0*	2.0	. . .	43.0	39.0	X	Hillsdale
III	C	Chalcedony	49.5	24.0	6.5	0	24.0	3.5*	. . .	17.0H	15.0	X	Lapeer
IV	A	Chert	48.0	20.0	5.0	23.0	17.0	3.0	X	14.0?	. . .	X	Washtenaw, Ann Arbor
IV	B	Chert	27.5	20.0	4.5	15.0	20.0	3.0	X	17.0H	16.0	. . .	Ionia
IV	D	Chert	42.5	18.0	6.0	20.0	14.5	3.0	X	21.0H	8.5	X	Washtenaw
V	..	Flint	120.0*	36.0	10.5	36.0	30.0	4.0	X	36.0	36.0	X	Washtenaw, Lodi Township
VI	A	Chert	36.0*	20.5	4.5	19.0	17.0	6.5	X	21.0H	18.0	X	Washtenaw
VI	B	Jasper	50.5	28.5	8.0	28.0	27.5	8.5	X	24.0H	24.0	X	Washtenaw
VIII	A	Chert	66.0	25.0	7.0	30.0	24.0	4.0	X	27.0H	21.0H	. . .	Allegan, Lee Township
VIII	B	Chert	46.0	25.0	7.5	8.0	25.0	5.5	. . .	26.0	. . .	X	Allegan, Lee Township
VIII	C	Chert	55.0	22.0	7.0	28.0	20.0	2.0	X	21.0	21.0	. . .	Berrien
IX	B	Chert	35.0	26.0	6.5	23.0	26.0	3.0	X	20.0	20.0	X	Berrien
IX	C	Chert	40.0*	19.0	3.0	0	17.5	3.0	. . .	32.0	. . .	. . .	Van Buren

*Dimension estimated; X signifies feature present, and H, hinge terminated.

frequently accompanied by fissure radiation from negative bulb areas, is characteristic.

Blade treatment shows a sometimes erratic flaking pattern marked along the edges by two to four large and fairly deep transverse scars per centimeter. These transverse flakes were removed by percussion methods which thus served to shape the projectile point prior to the drawing of the fluting channel spalls. There were probably two stages to this shaping process, after the flake-based blade had been drawn from its nucleus or core. Initial flaking by rough percussion technique served to thin and rudely shape the artifact. This was followed by more carefully executed percussion work to shape the blade outline, and it is this process which seems to be reflected by the transverse flake scars described above. The serrations resulting from this operation were pressed off, and the edges smoothed by removing, usually tiny triangular, flakes between the percussion scars along the ridges there defined.

Apices of these pressure-removed spalls are, of course, at the blade edges. All of the Michigan points indicate that fluting did not take place until the blade had thus been completed, although fine pressure trimming and edge grinding were most probably accomplished subsequently.

Two specific areas usually reflect more painstaking care: the tip and the basal sections. Tip definition, when not broken off and lost, exhibits greater care in the pressing off of fine, closely spaced, and sometimes even overlapping flakes than do the lateral edges below. Base and lateral edges extending from the tangs[1] up to perhaps the middle of the blade were ground smooth after completion of the flaking (and probably fluting) operations. This grinding does not appear to have been a function of mere friction with hafting materials, as some archaeologists suggest, since this phenomenon is frequently extreme and is altogether lacking on most later projectile point assemblages. It must, therefore, have been purposefully imposed before hafting took place—presumably

TABLE III

Measurements (in Millimeters) of Unbroken Fluted Points from Various Localities in Michigan

Data supplied by Harold W. Moll. The first seven specimens are in the Eldon S. Cornelius Collection. The remainder are in the collections of Sylvester Poltorak, A. L. Spooner, H. W. Moll, and Ida Yaggie.

Material	Length	Max. Width	Basal Width	Basal Depth	Fluting Scar Length		Provenience (County)
					Obverse	Reverse	
Chert?	52.0*	25.0	20.0	3.0	10.0	?	Midland, Porter Township
Flint	62.0	25.0	18.0	2.0	31.0	?	Mecosta, Hinton Township
Jasper	64.0	29.0	18.0	2.0	20.0	?	Tuscola
Chert	38.0	20.0	17.0	3.0	29.0	26.0	Midland, Porter Township
?	21.0	20.0	20.0	1.0	10.0	7.0	Midland, Edenville Township
Flint	39.0	20.0	20.0	3.0	16.0	8.0	Midland, Porter Township
Chert	45.0	27.0	?	1.0?	- -†	- -†	Midland, Porter Township
?	52.0	27.0	24.0	3.0	42.0	41.0	Saginaw, Tittabawassee
?	53.0	28.0	24.0	4.0	15.0	?	Newaygo
Jasper	76.0	30.0	27.0	3.0	39.0	39.0	Midland, Greendale Township
Jasper	85.0	32.0	23.0	6.0	40.0	?	Ottawa, Olive Township

*Dimension estimated.
†Fluting attempted on both faces, but hinged out immediately above the base.

[1] The term "tang" is employed in a nonfunctional sense to refer to the basally projecting lateral edges. If they are flared or expanded I have called them "ears" or "flared tangs."

TABLE IV

Measurements (in Millimeters) of Unbroken Fluted Points probably from Berrien County, Michigan

Data supplied by Amos R. Green. The specimens from Niles are in the Fort St. Joseph Museum at Niles. Those from Benton Harbor are in the collections of Harvey Franz and Amos Green. The single specimen from Bertrand Township comes from the Joel Gillette Collection and the last two from the George Franklin Collection. In accordance with the wishes of certain collectors, specific provenience information is not given. These specimens are not included in the tabulation of Points known to actually have come from Berrien County.

Length	Max. Width	Basal Width	Basal Depth	Fluting Scar Length		Provenience
				Obverse	Reverse	
48.0	25.0	?	3.0	20.0	15.0	near Niles
72.0	27.0	25.0	6.0	31.0	20.0	near Niles
64.0	21.0	20.0	4.0	31.0	25.0	near Niles
36.0	27.0	22.0	3.0	15.0	....	near Niles
30.0	26.0	25.0	?	16.0	15.0	near Niles
94.0	34.0	28.0	5.0	43.0	20.0	near Benton Harbor
60.0	24.0	19.0	3.5	19.0	....	near Benton Harbor
65.0	29.0	27.0	5.0	23.0	18.0	near Benton Harbor
56.0	22.0	22.0	3.5	28.0	19.0	near Benton Harbor
57.0	24.0	17.0	5.0	24.0	?	near Benton Harbor
53.0	20.0	19.0	2.5	20.0	?	near Benton Harbor
41.0	23.0	21.0	3.5	32.0	27.0	near Benton Harbor
38.0	21.5	21.5	2.5	11.0	?	near Benton Harbor
32.0	25.0	25.0	2.0	17.0	?	near Benton Harbor
57.0	29.0	?	?	25.0	?	near Benton Harbor
41.0	29.0	23.0	3.0	16.0	?	near Benton Harbor
62.0	31.0	26.0	4.0	30.0	27.0	Bertrand Township
22.0	17.0	17.0	4.0	8.0	....	Local provenience uncertain
35.0	21.0	?	2.5	12.0	....	Local provenience uncertain

to avoid cutting the lashings which probably held the projectile point to its shaft or foreshaft. It seems highly improbable that such grinding was the result of work-dulling (as though the artifact had been used as a knife or scraper), since grinding occurs only on those areas which were most likely lashed to a haft. In all cases of edge grinding, flake-back and other indications of edge wear and fatigue are characteristically absent. A study of the specimens suggests that the maximum limit of lateral grinding was roughly coextensive with the upper limits of the lashings which, it is thought, were the means by which the stone point was secured to its haft.

Reduction of basal edges to the concave form characteristic of fluted blades seems to have been largely a function of the fluting process and incidental to it, apart from pressure finishing and grinding. The Michigan data in this respect confirm the findings of John Witthoft in his study of the more specialized Enterline Chert Industry as exemplified at the Shoop site in eastern Pennsylvania (Witthoft, 1952:481-82). This is not to declare that basal depth and length of fluting are strictly correlated, for a deep and wide channel scar may be quite short, due to hinging not far from the striking platform. Aside from this common manifestation one may say, nevertheless, that length and, particularly, width and depth of a fluting scar do roughly reflect the depth of the basal concavity. Additionally, as has been intimated above, this concavity may be further accentuated by retouch and smoothing, but probably to only a minor extent.

TABLE V

Measurements (in Millimeters) of Unbroken Fluted Points from Cass County

Data supplied by George R. Fox. Information concerning the collectors was not forwarded.

Length	Max. Width	Basal Width	Basal Depth	Fluting Scar Length		Provenience (Township)
				Obverse	Reverse	
48.0	26.0	21.0	2.0	27.0	10.0	Jefferson
30.0	17.0	17.0	2.5	10.0	7.0	La Grange
33.0	22.0	22.0	3.0	11.0	....	La Grange
55.0	19.0	12.0	3.0	42.0	....	Newberg
42.0	28.0	25.0	3.0	25.0	....	North Porter
47.0	25.0	23.0	3.0	24.0	....	North Porter
80.0	25.0	18.0	4.0	64.0	35.0	Pokagon
70.0	25.0	20.0	5.0	65.0	....	Silver Creek
65.0	27.0	26.0	5.0	43.0	34.0	Volinia
31.0	20.0	20.0	2.5	17.0	15.0	Wayne
64.0	25.0	25.0	5.0	24.0	17.0	Wayne
64.0	26.0	26.0	5.5	23.0	17.0	Wayne
39.0	21.0	20.0	2.5	13.0	....	Wayne
28.0	25.0	25.0	3.5	12.0	12.0	Wayne
81.0	25.0	20.0	3.0	65.0	60.0	Unknown
54.0	19.0	14.0	2.0	43.0	....	Unknown
64.0	29.0	25.0	7.0	23.0	11.0	Unknown
48.0	26.0	22.0	2.0	26.0	....	Unknown

Fluting Techniques

One method of detaching channel flakes is clearly evident in the Michigan series, with a second technique possibly present in a few instances (see Figure 2). The first method may be described as preparation of the fluting striking platform by means of beveling the base. It appears that the original basal edge of the prefluted projectile point was straight, or even sometimes slightly convex. This edge was beveled over to the plane of one of the faces (probably by light percussion blows), and a striking platform was thus established. At this prepared point, a carefully directed blow detached the fluting spall from the face. Since this blow shattered parts of the edge, and the channel flake thus removed carried away with it the striking platform, the basal edge assumed a rough but definitely concave form. In order to flute the opposite face, the basal edge had to be reworked and beveled accordingly and a new striking platform prepared. In some instances the initial fluting so deepened the base or left such a deep negative bulb that fluting the opposite face was not feasible. Cross sections of such specimens at the base reveal a characteristically thin plano-concave or, more often, concavo-convex configuration. If the original fluting had not so negated the feasibility of bifacial fluting, a flute was then produced on the opposite face, further shattering and deepening the basal concavity. It is generally true that unifacially fluted specimens have shallower bases than do those upon which bifacial fluting has been successfully attempted. There are instances, certainly, where this generalization does not hold, but they are relatively infrequent among the fluted blades from Michigan and other areas with which I am familiar.

One may reasonably infer from the foregoing evidence that in all cases of differential fluting it was the cultural pattern to flute both faces of a projectile point, and that unifacial fluting was not a culturally "optional" alternative, but was technologically imposed by poorly controlled fluting on one face of the artifact. Another reason for the occurrence of some unifacially fluted specimens is obvious: the projectile point-to-be was broken during manufacture. After completion of the uni- or bifacially fluted point, the basal edge was trimmed by fine-pressure retouch. This was usually followed by pronounced grinding, not only at the base but also on tang edges and laterally up the blade, frequently as far as one-third or one-half the length of the whole artifact. A few examples from the Michigan collections have narrow but long flake scars, struck from the base, which impinge upon the main channel scar, apparently to widen the breadth of an unsatisfactory flute.

A second technique of fluting is suggested by a small number of Michigan specimens (Pl. III, B; Pl. VI, A and B). This is the technique of "triple channel-flake fluting" so carefully worked out by John Witthoft of the Pennsylvania State Museum in his study of the Enterline Chert Industry, in eastern Pennsylvania. By this method (see Figure 2), again starting with a straight or slightly convex basal edge, two parallel longitudinal channel spalls were detached, somewhat apart from each other,

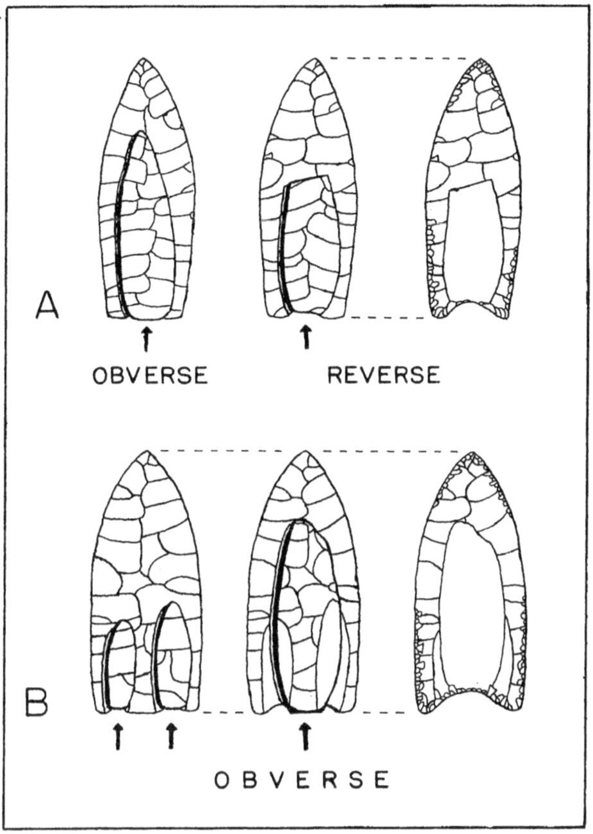

Fig. 2. Two Fluting Techniques Suggested by an Examination of Fluted Blades from Michigan.

A. Single channel flake removal from a beveled base.

B. Triple Channel Fluting (after Witthoft, 1952). Although only one face is represented, both faces are usually fluted in this manner. Note how basal configurations in A and B are a function of the fluting operation and subsequent retouch and grinding.

between the middle of the base and the lateral edges. In what has aptly been described as "applying core and blade technique to a bifaced tool" (Witthoft, 1952:483), these primary channel scars served to initially define the contours of the tangs and isolated, between them, a striking platform which served for the detachment of the main channel flake. Frequently, this method resulted in the total obliteration of the primary double channel scars, but sometimes the lower and outer portions of the scars survived the major fluting and retained the evidence upon which this interesting technique has been reconstructed. Witthoft suggested that the application of the triple channel-flake fluting procedure may account for many of the eastern fluted blades which exhibit two or more channel scars on the same face. This may be true in some cases and is well worth consideration. I would suggest that identification of this technique on the basis of just a few scattered points from other areas (otherwise not a clear part of the Enterline Industry, lithologically or on specific morphological details) must also take into account the probability that not all Paleo-Indian flint knappers were equally proficient. Many of the points showing multiple channel scars may really reflect subsequent attempts at fluting after the first had been somehow aborted. Witthoft certainly recognizes this possibility, and this may be the case with the few specimens from Michigan which suggest the Enterline technique. To fully resolve such questions a larger sample is needed and other data must be weighed.

Length of Fluting and Length of Fluting Scar—a Distinction

It will be noted that a distinction has been made in this study between "fluting length" and "fluting-scar length." This is an important distinction and one which warrants clarification. By "fluting-scar length" is meant the distance from the basal apex up to the greatest extremity of the fluting scar. Length of actual fluting, however, is herein determined by taking this dimension and adding to it the depth of the basal concavity. Since it has been established that fluting started at a distance from the tip, in large measure subsequently retained by the tangs or basal corners, this measurement procedure is verified by all of the fluted-blade assemblages with which I am directly familiar. Contours of the fluting scars on almost every one of these artifacts generally extend down the inside sectors of the tangs to a point well below that marked by the basal apex. Furthermore, the almost total absence of a negative bulb of percussion in the channel scar on one face of a fluted blade clearly indicates that the fluting blow was struck at a platform well below the finished apex of the base. Usually the opposite face exhibits a clear bulbar depression complemented by the concentric conchoidal ripple marks of the blow by which that channel flake had been detached (see Pl. II, A). The face upon which these features are seen was obviously fluted last.

These observations indicate that the basal edge of the prefluted projectile point was considerably more removed from the tip of the blade than is the trimmed and finished apex of the characteristic concave base. Fluting, therefore, actually began at this straight or somewhat convex edge and should be measured from that edge, which, though now removed, may generally be taken as a line connecting the extreme edges of the tangs. This distinction between fluting length and length of fluting scar has not been made explicit by most archaeologists. This can demonstrably lead to considerable discrepancies in comparing, for example, the fluting to blade-length percentages in two or more series of data compiled by different individuals, one of whom may have measured fluting length from the apex of the base, while the other may have obtained his figures by measuring up from a basal edge reconstructed as above. Such a discrepancy can be calculated when sufficient and pertinent measurements are presented and, especially, when photographs or drawings of the specimens involved, accompanied by a scale, are included in the reports. In all cases the distinction pointed out here should be made explicit.

Blade Configuration

To rigorously characterize the shapes of Michigan fluted points is somewhat difficult due to nuances of form. This information may better be gained by an examination of the plates and outline drawings given. In general, however, the series grades from parallel-sided forms, with greatest width at or close to the middle of the blade and with edges descending straight or nearly so from this point to the basal tangs, to specimens exhibiting convex edges curving gradually to the base. The latter may or may not show incipient expansion at the base; if they do, there is slight constriction of the blade, obviously, just above the tangs or basal ears. Some of these could fit into the tentative classification "Ohio Fluted," as it is defined by Krieger (1947) and Wormington (1949: 33-35), and others, following the attempt at a standardization of nomenclature made at the symposium held in September, 1941, at Santa Fe, New Mexico (see p. 40). Michigan examples usually do not exhibit the flaring or expanded basal ears (but see Fig. 1, L; Pl. II, B and D). Others in the sample from Michigan are quasi-triangular in outline (Pl. I, B).

A few of the Michigan fluted blades (Pl. VI, A, for example) are decidedly ovoid, with relatively deep bases and a resulting emphasis of the tangs. Some of the points show evidence of breakage and reworking (Pl. IV, B); others bear indications of secondary employment as knives (Pl. V).

Cross sections at the base are variable rather than uniform, but more frequently have a biconcave or lenticular configuration, since the majority of specimens are fluted on both faces. There is one example of a plano-concave basal cross section, and this seems to be the result of retention of an original flake facet on one face and of fluting on the other. A few points, again unifacially fluted, have a concavo-convex form. Above the maximum extent of fluting, blade cross sections are typically ovoid or biconvex rather than flat.

Fluted blades from Michigan may be characterized as usually heavy and thick, and they show relatively little evidence of thinning the blade aside from the actual fluting. The transverse flaking pattern is apt to be haphazard and poorly controlled, and fluting, often terminated abruptly by hinge fracture, rarely runs the full length of the artifact. Size is extremely variable within a length range of from 21.0 mm. to 120.0 mm. and with an average length of 53.0 mm. for 69 measured specimens. Lateral and basal edge grinding is almost universal in the sample.

The petrology of specimens, where known for certain, has been presented in the descriptive tables. The majority of them are manufactured from a rather poor quality chert, usually gray, a common variety of siliceous material native to the region. In all characteristics, but particular varieties of material, the Michigan sample is comparable to most fluted-blade series in the Northeast with which I am familiar. Possible exceptions, depending upon the criteria selected for comparison, are the uniform Enterline Chert Industry, certain exotic forms from Ohio and Virginia, and the terminal Paleo-Indian Period complex represented at the Reagen site in Vermont. These observations will be refined further on in this paper.

REVIEW OF GEOCHRONOLOGY OF LOWER PENINSULA OF MICHIGAN AND OF ADJACENT GREAT LAKES BASINS

This review of the geochronology of the Michigan area has been obtained from many sources, but principally from Leverett and Taylor, 1915; Bretz, 1951a; Hough, 1953; Melhorn, 1954; Martin, 1955; Zumberge and Potzger, 1955 and 1956; Zumberge, 1956; Flint, 1956; and Leighton, 1957. As anyone even remotely concerned with Late Pleistocene geochronology will realize, the body of complex and ever-accumulating data in this province is voluminous, and interpretations based on those data are frequently at variance on several important points. Use of radiocarbon age determinations has been exceedingly fruitful of late and has permitted correlations of past geologic events on an increasingly finer scale of tolerance. From this complex and often contradictory array of data and theory, I have constructed a geochronology that is selectively hybridized from the work of many geologists. This should reflect the probable sequence of major events, at least as presently understood. Some details may be changed in the future, but it seems unlikely that the main outlines will be seriously altered. Since the archaeologist's only means at present for dating Paleo-Indian manifestations in this region, aside from typology, rests upon geological associations, it is felt that an attempt at correlation is warranted, however tentative the conclusions. The reader should make allowances for the frequent qualifications which follow, realizing their necessity when one is dealing with a complex of closely interwoven fact and inference.[2]

Cary Subage

Because the Wisconsin ice sheet in Michigan or, more exactly, the ice lobes of the adjacent Great Lakes basins, completely covered the state during the Cary Maximum and extended southward into Ohio, Indiana, and Illinois, it is clear that the maximum age of all fluted blades found in Michigan is limited by the presence of the early Cary ice. The areas in which these projectile points have been discovered were not ice-free and, hence, were not open to human penetration until after the

[2]For a broader and less specific attempt by another archaeologist to evaluate geological and paleogeographical information and theory for archaeological use, see George I. Quimby's provocative paper (1954). The reader's attention is also invited to a paper by James B. Griffin, which deals with the correspondence of independent absolute and relative time indicators in archaeology, geology, paleontology, and radiocarbon age determinations (Griffin, 1956).

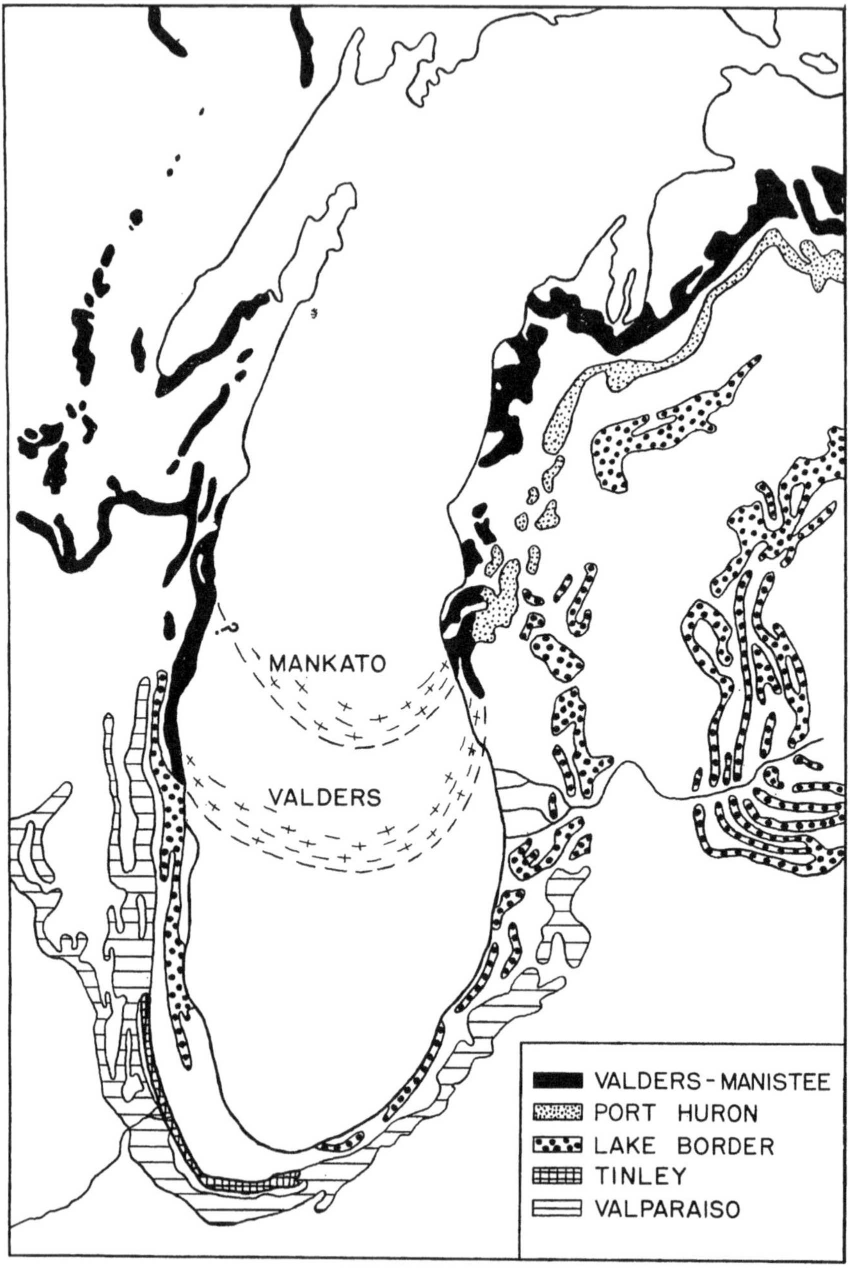

Map 2. Major Late Pleistocene morainic systems of the Lake Michigan lobe of the Wisconsin ice sheet. The Valders-Manistee is Valders in origin; the Port Huron moraine (and the Manistee where conformable) is Mankato; the Lake Border system is Late Cary; both the Tinley and Valparaiso moraines are Middle Cary features. Modified from Bretz, 1951a: 426, Fig. 1.

Cary recession began. Accordingly, this brief account of the geochronology involved begins with the early retreat of the Cary from the southern part of the Lower Peninsula of Michigan.

The extensive Valparaiso morainic system, a Middle Cary feature (see Zumberge, 1956:3 and 7), can be traced from southeastern Wisconsin, around the southern shores of Lake Michigan (though well inland) through Illinois and Indiana, to southwestern Michigan (Bretz, 1951a: Fig. 1; also see Map 2 herein). After the retreat of the Cary ice from this position, there followed a short readvance of the Lake Michigan lobe, the lobe which built the Tinley moraine. A later readvance in Late Cary times built the Lake Border moraine. Retreat of the ice from the Tinley position led to the birth of Glacial Lake Chicago, with a water plane gradually rising to the Glenwood stage of 640 feet above present mean sea level (Bretz, 1951a:404-7; Melhorn, 1954). The stages of Glacial Lake Chicago have been well established and the following summarizes this history:

> Glacial Lake Chicago existed in the Lake Michigan basin in front of a retreating lobe of the Wisconsin ice sheet and discharged to the Illinois River, an affluent of the Mississippi. Its three groups of shore lines record three different stages of essentially static level, separated by two stages of relatively rapid lowering from one level to another. With only one exception, all who have studied the lake's history consider that the highest stage was the earliest and the lowest the latest, that each static stage was determined by minimum erosion on the channel floor at the head of the outlet, and that each drop in lake level was caused by fairly rapid deepening at the channel head.
>
> The landward margin of Lake Chicago was the Valparaiso moraine system [the dam, however, was the Tinley moraine, Bretz, 1951a: 425] which loops around the southern end of the basin in the familiar Wisconsin lobate habit [see Map 2]. Two low places in this moraine became simultaneous discharge ways, converging to become one a few miles down stream. Both continued to function during nearly forty feet of deepening from the highest (Glenwood) to the lowest (Toleston) stage of the lake. The intermediate (Calumet) shore line lies approximately in the middle of this vertical interval. (Bretz, 1951a: 401-2)

Thus, with the retreat of the Cary ice into southern and central Michigan, earliest Glacial Lake Chicago was born. Possibly sometime prior to 14,000 years ago (see Zumberge and Potzger, 1956:277, and read Mankato for "Cary") this body of glacial melt water had already reached its subsequently long-lived Glenwood stage with the Tinley moraine acting as its dam. At approximately the same time Lake Maumee, which attained a level of 790 feet A. T. (above present mean sea level), had developed in the area of the basins of modern Lake Huron and Lake Erie. By about 13,600 B. P. (before the present), Lake Arkona and Early Lake Saginaw filled or partly filled the area formerly beneath the waters of Lake Maumee, and the Glenwood stage of Lake Chicago continued to occupy the southern portions of the Lake Michigan Basin (see Hough, 1953; Flint, 1956 and 1957:342-9; and Zumberge and Potzger, 1956). With the withdrawal of the Cary ice the southern part of Michigan was never again glaciated, except in the area from Saginaw Bay to about halfway between the southern end of Lake Huron and Lake St. Clair in

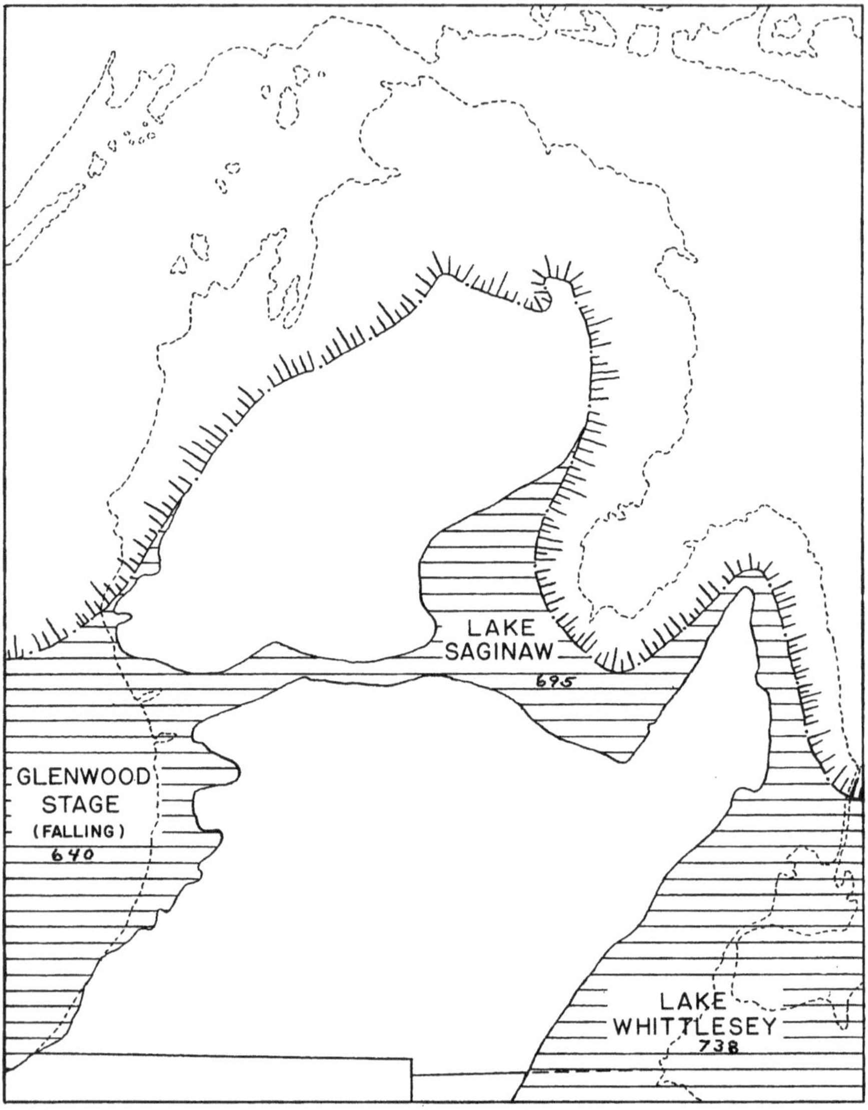

Map 3. Michigan during the Mankato Maximum. The outwash channel connecting Lake Saginaw with the Glenwood Stage of Glacial Lake Chicago actually represents what were probably meandering streams. Revised from Bretz, 1951a and b; Hough, 1953; Leverett and Taylor, 1915; Martin, 1955; and Zumberge, 1956.

the east during the Mankato Maximum. The retreats of the various ice sheets were not a process of continual withdrawal by steady ablation, but were most likely characterized by fluctuations of the ice fronts, the cumulative result of which was general retreat.

Mankato Subage

The Straits of Mackinac remained ice-blocked, and partly through this region there developed a readvance of the Wisconsin ice which reached its culmination with the Mankato Maximum, now correlated with the Port Huron morainic system and estimated to date, by radiocarbon, at around 12,400 B. P. (see Flint, 1956, and Leighton, 1957). To allay possible confusion concerning this correlation, it should be mentioned that as late as 1956 most glacial geologists had attributed the Port Huron moraine to the Late Cary. Recent information has revised this assignment and has correlated the moraine with the Mankato Maximum (Leighton, 1957, and Leighton and Wright, 1957; see also Flint's discussion, 1956:275). Hough and Zumberge have accepted the revision (verbal communications). In this work the Mankato is thus correlated with the Port Huron and the Manistee moraines, where conformable (Leighton, 1957:109).

Contemporaneous with the Mankato Maximum (Map 3), the Glenwood stage of Glacial Lake Chicago continued its occupancy of the Lake Michigan Basin, but with a now falling water level. Lakes Whittlesey (738 feet A. T. and draining north to Lake Saginaw) and Saginaw (695 feet A. T.) were at the same time extant in the basins of what are now the modern lakes Huron and Erie. Lake Saginaw was connected to Lake Chicago by a broad outlet channel—the Grand River Outlet—which ran across the center of the Lower Peninsula, separating the ice-free regions to the north from those to the south. With the later retreat of the Mankato from its Port Huron front, lake levels dropped somewhat from their former elevations. Thus, by about 12,000 years ago First Lake Warren stood between 690 and 682 feet above sea level in this area, and the first attained Calumet stage of Lake Chicago (620 feet A. T.) was roughly contemporaneous (Bretz, 1951a:408). Our first real glimpse, by pollen analysis, of the climatic and biotic conditions that prevailed in southern Michigan relate to this time: cool and moist climate was correlated with probably scattered copses of spruce and fir trees (Zumberge and Potzger, 1955 and 1956). Little is directly known of the contemporaneous fauna except that mammoth were present, dated "by means of wood associated with the Jefferson mammoth in Tompkins Township, Jackson County, Michigan. This wood dates 12,200 ± 700 (M-507)" (Griffin, 1956:18).

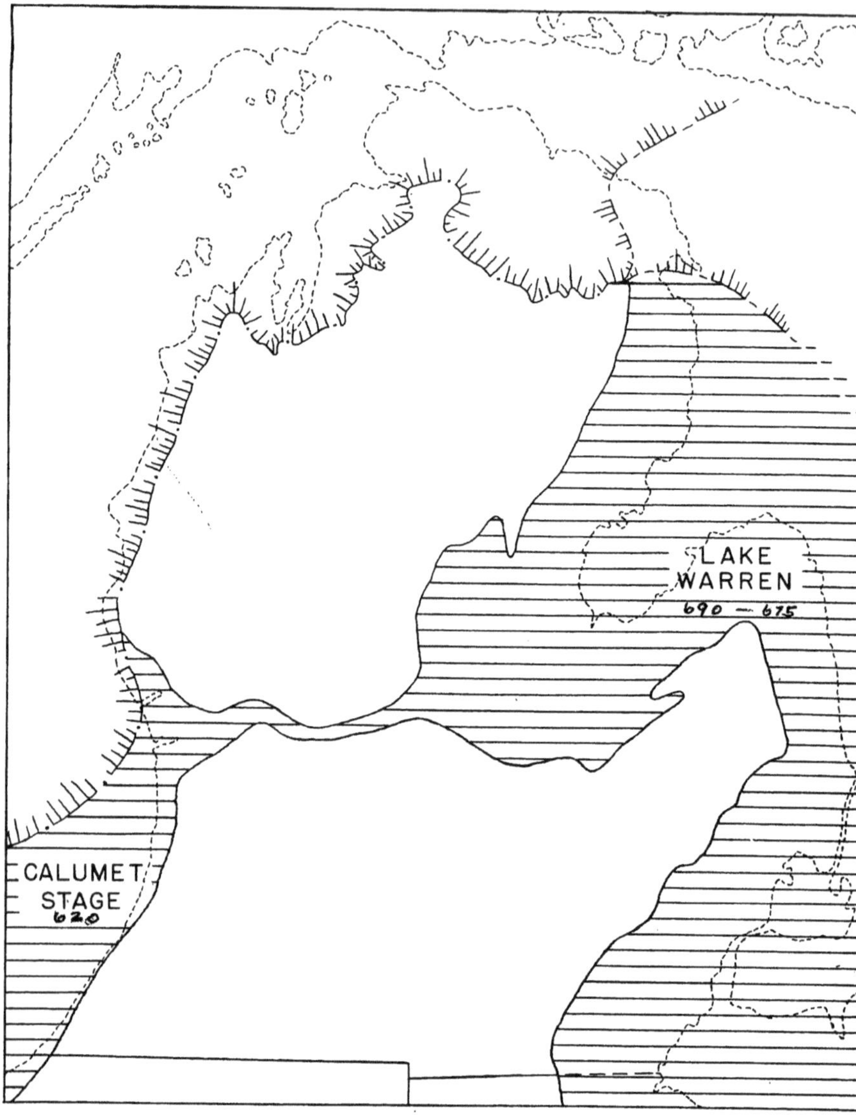

Map 4. Michigan during the Valders Maximum. Revised from Bretz, 1951a and b; Hough, 1953; Leverett and Taylor, 1915; Martin, 1955; and Zumberge, 1956.

Two Creeks Interstadial

Between the end of the Mankato retreat and the next and last glacial advance, there intervened a period of low water, here provisionally identified as the Bowmanville stage,[3] during which greatly shrunken and isolated lakes seem to have stood in the basins of lakes Michigan, Huron, and Erie. The northern and southern sectors of the Lower Peninsula of Michigan were fully connected by dry land. This period is called in the Wisconsin sequence the Two Creeks Interstadial. It probably began shortly after 12,000 years ago and lasted until about 11,000 B. P. (see description of radiocarbon sample M-288a, which dates the Bowmanville at 11,200 ± 600 or between 11,800 and 10,600 B. P., (Crane, 1956; see also Zumberge and Potzger, 1956:277). This and some later periods are well documented by stratigraphic and other physical evidence, especially in eastern Wisconsin, and by radiocarbon dates obtained therefrom (Flint, 1956:267-75). This material is amplified and expanded upwards in time to beyond the postglacial Xerothermic or Altithermal by stratigraphic, beach strand, and pollen studies, reinforced by radiocarbon dating, from southwestern Michigan (Zumberge and Potzger, 1955 and 1956).

Lake levels rose again during the later phases of the Two Creeks Interstadial, and by about 11,300 B. P. (time established by radiocarbon), had drowned a forest at the type locality of Two Creeks, Wisconsin (Zumberge and Potzger, 1956:277-79).[4] Shortly after this event the drowned forest was pushed over and buried beneath the characteristic red till of the Valders advance. Subsequently, lake sediments were deposited on top of this till.

Valders Subage

The Valders Maximum (Map 4) seems to be securely dated at around 10,700 B. P. and is correlated with the red drift in Wisconsin and Michigan and with such relatively small moraines as the Whitehall (see proposed ice fronts in Leighton, 1957:110, Fig. 1). Pollen data from the Hartford Bog and South Haven profiles in the southwestern part of the state indicate a moist and cool to cold climate. Once again the Grand River outlet was active. Real tundra conditions, if present at all, were most likely confined to the ice border areas, but extensive inland lakes, bogs, and swamps must have dominated large areas in the northern

---

[3] The assignment of the name "Bowmanville" to the low-water stage correlative with Two Creeks may change in the future. Zumberge has informed me that the name may be reapplied because of difficulties of correlating the type locality. This affects the label only, of course, and not the phenomenon here described.

[4] "At the moment, the Two Creeks forest bed is considered to represent a period of ice recession of sufficient magnitude to permit the opening of the Straits of Mackinac, thus causing the discharge of Glacial Lake Chicago to shift from the Chicago outlet (Des Plaines River) to an unknown eastern outlet" (Zumberge, 1956: 4).

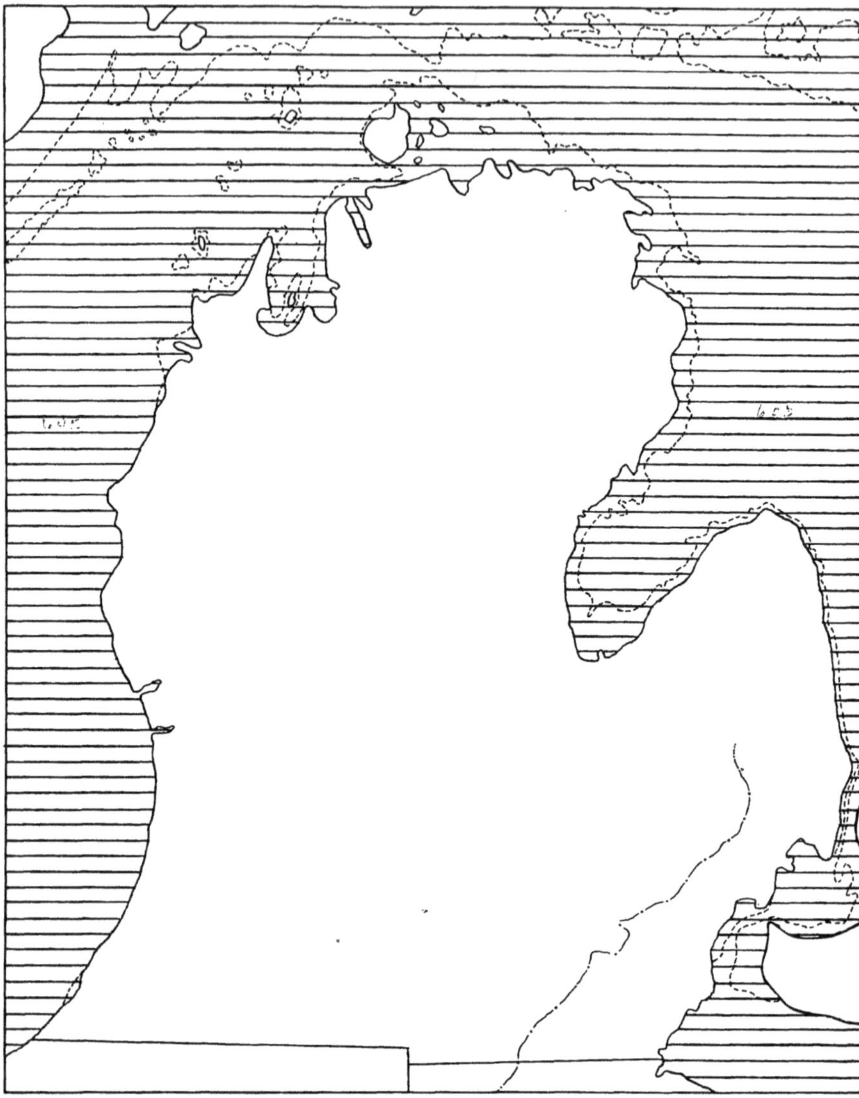

Map 5. Michigan during the Algonquin Lake stage. Interrupted line indicates remnants of the Lake Maumee shore line. Revised from Hough, 1953; Leverett and Taylor, 1915; and Martin, 1955.

sections of "open" land. Coeval with, or shortly after, the Valders Maximum a 620 feet A. T. water plane had developed in the Lake Michigan Basin (Calumet stage of later Glacial Lake Chicago).

The earliest extensive impounding of melt water in the Huron-Erie basins during this time was manifested by Glacial Lake Wayne (655 feet A. T.). It was succeeded by Lake Warren (675 feet A. T.). Drainage was again from the Huron-Erie basins to the Lake Michigan Basin and then out through the Des Plaines outlet channel.

Post-Valders Maximum

Between 10,000 and 9,500 years ago the Valders retreat had commenced and the spruce-fir forestation of lower Michigan, as revealed through pollen analyses of the South Haven and Hartford Bog profiles, was declining. That mastodon were a part of the ecology at this time level is suggested by a tusk from Lenawee County, radiocarbon dated at the University of Michigan (Crane, 1956: Sample M-282). By this time, too, Glacial Lake Chicago stood at its Toleston stage of 605 feet above sea level, and Lakes Grassmere (640 feet A. T.) and Lundy (620 feet A. T.) were extant in the eastern Michigan and southwestern Ontario area. The Straits of Mackinac were open by 8,500 B. P., and Lake Algonquin, at 605 feet, now occupied the basins of lakes Michigan and Huron, and may have lasted until about 7,900 B. P., although with a falling water plane (Crane, 1956: Sample M-288). Lake Erie seems to have been cut off from this great lake, and its contemporaneous stage is called simply "Lake Erie" (573 feet A. T.).

Hough has recently revised some of his glacial lake correlations across the Lower Peninsula of Michigan. He has suggested that the Grassmere, Lundy, and early Algonquin stages in the Huron and Erie basins were correlatives of the Glenwood, Calumet, and Toleston stages, respectively, in the Lake Michigan Basin (Hough, 1956). I believe that the correlations indicated in this section and in Table VII are more generally held by Pleistocene geologists. Hough's interesting new proposals are mentioned to show that the correlation problem is by no means completely solved.

With the Lake Algonquin stage the Lower Peninsula was entirely open to human exploitation, with but relatively little flooding and submergence of its modern shores except for the far north (Map 5). The Grand River outlet formerly connecting the large lake bodies in the east and west had earlier disappeared. Lake Algonquin discharged through the Chicago outlet and the St. Clair-Detroit River channels. Temperatures continued to rise, although a generally wet climate prevailed in northern Michigan (Spurr and Zumberge, 1956:102). Jack pine forest cover gradually gave way to pine about 6,000 years ago, at which time Lake Payette lay in the Michigan and Huron basins with a water plane of 415 feet above sea level, and Lake Erie was now, as during Lake Algonquin times and thereafter, at its present elevation. The mastodon may possibly have survived in the area to this late date, if the radiocarbon age determination of 6,300 ± 500 B. P. for a mastodon tusk from Washtenaw County is a reliable one (Crane, 1956: Sample M-67). Such a late date for the survival of this important representative of Pleistocene fauna seems insecure on the basis of a single radiocarbon date, especially since acid-soluble carbonates were used for the sample. Nevertheless, the possibility should be noted. Almost contemporaneous, it seems, were caribou, dated at 5,870 ± 400 B. P., from a locality near Flint (Crane, 1956: Sample M-294).[5]

Xerothermic and Post-Xerothermic

The decline in lake levels already noted continued until about 5,000 years ago, when Lake Chippewa stood at only 230 feet A. T. in the Lake Michigan Basin, and Lake Stanley at the same time manifested a water plane of 180 feet A. T. in the Lake Huron Basin. This decline in lake levels was a consequence of further retreat of the Wisconsin ice. The ice forming the northern dam of Lake Algonquin retreated to North Bay, Ontario, thus opening a low outlet which resulted in a lowering of water planes. Lake Chippewa was connected to Lake Stanley through the Straits of Mackinac and drainage continued through the North Bay outlet (Zumberge, 1956:8).

Forests of pine were by now giving way to a mixed pine and deciduous population, largely of oak, in an increasingly warming habitat, as revealed by the pollen profiles in southwestern Michigan. By 4,000 years ago, the Chippewa-Nipissing transition had clearly developed (Zumberge and Potzger, 1956:277). Zumberge has recently stated that "Uplift of the North Bay outlet caused the water to rise in the Michigan and Huron basins back to the controlling level of the old southern outlets at 605′ A. T." (1956:8).

Coincident with the Xerothermic (also called Altithermal, Hypsithermal, or Post-Glacial Climatic Optimum) at about 3,500 B. P., the Nipissing Great Lakes attained a level of 605 feet A. T. in the Lakes Michigan and Huron depressions. Lake Erie continued as a separate body of water maintained at the modern 573-foot level. Obviously, this was a period of warm and dry climate. Indeed, it is characterized by Spurr and Zumberge (1956:103) as being semiarid, at least in the northern sectors of the lower Michigan peninsula. In the southwestern quarter of the state, forests at this time were of mixed oak, hickory, and pine (Zumberge and Potzger, 1956:281-86).

Largely on the basis of information inferred from varve chronology, and somewhat different views on glacier retreat, Antevs placed this period before 4,500 and after 7,000 B. P. (Antevs, 1953, 1954, and 1955). He has since revised his estimate upwards in time (Antevs, 1957).

[5]For a recent discussion of the survival of the mastodon into Late Pleistocene-Early Recent times, see Williams (1957).

TABLE VI

Late Pleistocene Geologic Time Divisions

The Cochrane, as a definite Wisconsin glacial ice stage, is confined to Canada and is not represented in Michigan. Vertical scale in this table has been foreshortened.

HOLOCENE or RECENT		
LATE PLEISTOCENE	WISCONSIN	Cochrane Valders (Two Creeks) Mankato Cary Tazewell Iowan Farmdale
	SANGAMON INTERGLACIAL	
	ILLINOIAN	
	YARMOUTH INTERGLACIAL	

Flint, on the other hand, has placed the Xerothermic somewhere between 4,500 and 5,500 years ago (Flint, 1956:272). I have followed Zumberge and Potzger's placement of this period at 3,500 B. P. as more compatible with the Hartford Bog and South Haven pollen profiles in southwestern Michigan and with the applicable radiocarbon dates (Zumberge and Potzger, 1956:280; and Zumberge, 1956:7).[6]

[6] Antevs has consistently preferred varve chronology over radiocarbon and, although his estimate of the age of the Nipissing is now more in line with that generally accepted today by geologists, his pre-Nipissing chronology demands a much greater time depth than radiocarbon alone will allow. He has recently written: "Important dates in this approximate North American varve chronology [his own] are as follows: about 10,700 years for the Cochrane oscillations; 13,800 for the end of the Pembroke halt and the opening of the North Bay outlet; 18,500 for the Valders (Mankato) glacial maximum at Milwaukee; 19,000 for the Two Creeks forest bed; and about 19,500 years for the comparatively warm Hanover age" (Antevs, 1957: 129). The implications of this chronology, if valid, have obvious and interesting bearing on archaeology. Griffin, in discussing this problem, has observed that "If Antev's chronology for the glacial recession were correct, it should be possible to find fluted blades in all of northern Wisconsin, Michigan, Minnesota and well up to the Cochrane area in eastern Ontario and north of Lake Nipigon" (Griffin, 1956, p. 21). Fluted blades have not been reported from any of these areas.

Oak-pine forestation and cooler climates were prevalent by about 2,500 B. P. and the Nipissing Great Lakes were succeeded by the Algoma waters, with a drop in level to 595 feet A. T. due to downcutting of the St. Clair River at the Port Huron outlet. Today the water planes stand in Lake Michigan and Lake Huron at 581 feet and in Lake Erie at 573 feet.

This examination of Late Pleistocene events in the lower Michigan peninsula and surrounding Great Lakes basins is summarized in Tables VI and VII. Brief as the foregoing has necessarily been, we now turn to an analysis of the Michigan fluted points and their placement in a time continuum.

Since the manuscript for this monograph was submitted to the University of Michigan Press in June, 1957, two new publications relating to the archaeology and geochronology of the Paleo-Indian Period have appeared (Ritchie, 1957, and Quimby, 1958). References have been made to the study on which Quimby's paper is based (pp. 2 and 37), and substantial agreement obtains between my remarks and those in his published report. Ritchie's investigations are mentioned in the footnote on page 39, and his published conclusions do not depart from his earlier statements as briefly intimated there. Quimby's conclusions, based on geochronological correlation of 6 fluted-point loci in the Lake Michigan Basin, are fairly close to those I give, which are on the basis of a much larger collection of data. Both studies present evidence in some opposition to the conclusions of Ritchie in New York State, and reflect the difficulties in correlating the Upper Great Lakes with the Northeastern sequence. Since the geological picture is clearer and more detailed in the former region, it is felt that the dates suggested by geologists for Ritchie's data will eventually be pushed backwards in time and will become more compatible with those I suggest. After all, New York State and Michigan are not far removed in space and it seems likely that major cultural and climato-ecological developments in both areas will prove to have been fairly synchronous.

TABLE VII

Late Pleistocene Geochronology in Michigan
and in the Basins of Lakes Michigan, Huron, and Erie

The absolute chronology is based on radiocarbon data. Compiled and modified from Bretz, 1951a; Flint, 1956; Hough, 1953; Leighton, 1957; Leverett and Taylor, 1915; Zumberge, 1956; Zumberge and Potzger, 1956.

YEARS B. P.	WISCONSIN CHRONOLOGY	FORESTATION & CLIMATE	GLACIAL LAKE STAGES IN BASINS OF L. MICHIGAN	L. HURON & L. ERIE
0			LAKE MICHIGAN (580)	LAKE HURON (580) & LAKE ERIE (573)
1000				
2000		OAK-PINE (COOLER)	ALGOMA (595)	ALGOMA & ERIE
3000	XEROTHERMIC	OAK-HICKORY-PINE (WARM & DRY)	NIPISSING (605) TRANSITION	NIPISSING & ERIE
4000				
5000		OAK-PINE (WARMING)	CHIPPEWA (230)	STANLEY (180) & ERIE
6000		PINE (WARMING)	PAYETTE (415)	PAYETTE & ERIE
7000		JACK PINE (WARMING)		
8000	ICE	(WET)	ALGONQUIN (605)	ALGONQUIN & ERIE
9000	RETREAT	SPRUCE-FIR (DECLINE)	TOLESTON (605)	GRASSMERE (640) & LUNDY (620)
10,000	VALDERS MAXIMUM (RED TILL)	(COLD & MOIST)	CALUMET (620)	SECOND L. WARREN (675)
11,000	TWO CREEKS INTERSTADIAL		BOWMANVILLE (580-)	FIRST L. ERIE (SEPARATE LAKE IN HURON BASIN)
12,000	MANKATO MAX. (PORT HURON)	SPRUCE-FIR	FIRST CALUMET (620) GLENWOOD (640)	FIRST L. WARREN (690-) L. SAGINAW (695) WHITTLESEY (738)
13,000			GLENWOOD	EARLY L. SAGINAW ARKONA (710-695)
14,000	LATE CARY (LAKE BORDER SYSTEM)			
?	MIDDLE CARY (VALPARAISO, TINLEY, & DEFIANCE) CARY MAXIMUM		GLENWOOD (640) NO LAKES	LAKE MAUMEE (790) NO LAKES

SUGGESTED CORRELATIONS OF FLUTED BLADE LOCI AND LATE PLEISTOCENE EVENTS

In this section I have relied heavily upon the mapping of Late Pleistocene features found in Leverett and Taylor, 1915; Bretz, 1951a; Hough, 1953; Melhorn, 1954; and Martin, 1955 (which is largely an adaptation of Leverett and Taylor). Sole reliance has not been placed upon modern elevation data in attempting to correlate the loci of fluted-blade finds with past geologic features, because of such poorly understood variables as small hinge lines and differential uplift and subsidence, phenomena which, even if well known, I am not equipped to handle. The plotting of the archaeological finds against the geological maps, plus the employment of elevational data, have constituted the basic methodology upon which the following correlations are founded.

Berrien and Cass Counties

Berrien County lies in the extreme southwestern corner of Michigan and is bordered on the north and northeast by Van Buren County and on the east by Cass County (Map 1). The southern border is defined by the Michigan-Indiana state line, and the county faces west on Lake Michigan. Of the 29 fluted blades known to have been found in Berrien County, provenience data of a site-specific nature is limited to relatively few. The greater part of my information on this material has been procured from Amos R. Green, of Eau Claire, who has made an archaeological survey of the county in recent years and has incorporated some of his findings in an unpublished report (Green, ms). I have had the privilege of reading and abstracting this manuscript and have benefited from correspondence and conversation with its author.

While specific locations are not known for most of the fluted points from Berrien County, Green has established that they were all discovered on farms in Berrien, Oronoko, Pipestone, Niles, and Sodus townships, with the possible exceptions of those known only from "near Benton Harbor." This indicates a marked concentration of fluted points in the eastern part of the county, a distribution which is compatible with the distributional situation in Cass County reported (through correspondence) by George R. Fox, of Dowagiac, who has also been engaged in site-survey work in southwestern Michigan. Estimates of the earliest possible entry of man into Michigan must be largely based upon the finds made in this area because of the pattern of glacier retreat in the state.

According to Green, no fluted blades have been discovered in Berrien County below an elevation of approximately 660 feet above sea level. Specifically, he cites two loci as being above the 720-foot contour, seven above the 700-foot contour, two above 680 feet, and one above the 660-foot contour (Green, ms, p. 4). This last-mentioned locality is the Moccasin Bluff site which is situated on a terrace of the

St. Joseph River near Buchanan. The terrace formation on which the site is located actually grades upward from an elevation of about 640 to a little over 660 feet (Quimby, verbal communication). Unlike the Paleo-Indian material, the sites of later peoples occur well below the 640-foot contour in Berrien County. Some of the finds of fluted points in the St. Joseph River area are near the shore remnants of a glacial lake which was confined between the Lake Border and Valparaiso moraines, which are Late and Middle Cary features, respectively. This inland lake may have had a water plane as high as 660 feet A. T., and it later became a bay of Glacial Lake Chicago with a lower water plane (Leverett and Taylor, 1915:226). The lake must be somewhat younger than the moraines which contained it, and it may be as old as Late Cary, deriving its waters in large part from the ablating ice as it retreated from its Lake Border position (Map 2). If this reconstruction is correct, the lake was a Late Cary feature and correlative with the Glenwood stage of Lake Chicago and thus should date between 14,000 B. P. at the earliest and about 12,500 B. P. at the latest—if, indeed, it survived as late as the Mankato Maximum. Leverett and Taylor (1915:225-26) suggest that the lake was contemporaneous with the final building of the Lake Border moraine. If their correlation is valid, the age of the lake must be closer to 14,000 than to 12,500 B. P. The fluted points in this area, then, cannot antedate Middle Cary features but may be as old as Late Cary. Their makers, on geochronological grounds, could also have been in the area at any time after this. Elevational data (no fluted points have been found below 660 to 640 feet) indicate that Paleo-Indians were probably in the area at the same time as the Late Cary inland lake. If they were there later, it is strange that not one shred of evidence has been found at lower elevations. A maximum date for the earliest penetration of Early Man into Berrien County can be suggested with some justification. Circa 13,500 B. P. seems most probable.

Eastward, fluted projectile points in Cass County have been found in a scattered distribution over an area less rich in Cary and post-Cary features. Nevertheless, George R. Fox has indicated (in correspondence) that a few fluted points have been found near the shore lines of an old glacial lake (Lake Dowagiac) which cut into the western part of the county. This lake could have been older than the one just described in Berrien County, since its locality was uncovered somewhat earlier by the receding Cary ice. Although it is not known when this lake became extinct, it seems doubtful that it lasted until Mankato times. It was certainly extinct by Bowmanville (Two Creeks) times. However, the bulk of Cass County fluted points have been found right on the bed of this lake, and those seemingly associated with its shores are most likely later in age and perhaps contemporaneous with the Berrien County specimens. After the retreat of the Cary ice, this entire area was never again extensively subjected to impounded melt-water lakes.

Descriptions of some of the artifacts from Berrien and Cass Counties have been presented in Tables IV and V and outline drawings of some of the Cass County specimens are shown in Figure 1. Two complete points from Berrien County are illustrated (Plates VIII, C and IX, B). In the Museum of Anthropology are three interesting basal fragments from the Moccasin Bluff site (Pl. VII, B, C, and D), which were collected by John C. Birdsell. Another basal piece is also described here, since it is included on the same plate as the Moccasin Bluff fragments. This is a specimen found in Goodland Township, Lapeer County, by Carman Baggerly (Pl. VII, A). Since these artifacts are too fragmentary to facilitate their inclusion in the tables, yet are still of some interest, a brief description is in order.

Two of the basal fragments are made of a variegated grayish white flint and two of gray chert. Of the flint specimens, one has a basal width of 27.0 mm. and a basal depth of 6.0 mm. It is bifacially fluted with a single channel scar exhibited in each instance, one of which scars is pronouncedly rippled. The other specimen is 20.5 mm. wide at the base and has a basal concavity of 4.5 mm. Maximum width of the blade seems to have been about 22.0 mm., and near the middle of the projectile point. Its maximum thickness, 7.5 mm., occurs here too. Tangs are pronounced. Both artifacts are heavily ground on the edges.

Of the chert specimens, basal width and depth dimensions are 20.5 and 5.5 mm., and 23.5 and 2.5 mm., respectively. One is fluted on both faces by single and double channel flake removals. It is heavily ground basally and laterally up to the break. The other point, that from Lapeer County, in many ways the most interesting, is unifacially fluted. The retention of the original flake facet on one face has resulted in a pseudo-flute. The basal edge had been beveled over to the plane of the opposite face, and the flute then struck from the striking platform thus prepared.

Washtenaw County

Twelve fluted points from Washtenaw County in southeastern Michigan are in the Museum of Anthropology collections. Of these, specific proveniences are known for only five: two are from Ann Arbor, two are from Salem, and one is from Lodi Township. Immediately to the east of these find areas is a long series of successive glacial lake beaches (Martin, 1955). The closest of these remnants are those of Lake Maumee, the first and most extensive lake body to occupy this region in post-Cary Maximum times. Several beaches of successive water planes of Lake Arkona lie just east of the Maumee shore, which they roughly parallel. Also in the area are traces of Lake Whittlesey. Since all of these beaches are within less than two and a half miles of each other in certain places and are likewise frequently close to later lake shores, for example, Wayne, Warren, and so forth, to the east, an attempt to correlate any one of them with the archaeological material must be suspect. Nevertheless, the presence of five fluted points in a fairly restricted area along the landward side of these early lakes is strong evidence of a correlative and not a chance relationship. I would suggest that a temporal correlation may be assumed with one or several of these beaches and that the fluted blades may be contemporaneous with those from the southwestern corner of the state. They may date, of course, any time after the Middle Cary, but their possible association with remnant features of Lakes Maumee-Arkona-Whittlesey (*ca.* 14,500 to 12,500 B. P.), coupled with indications of an early Paleo-Indian penetration in the southwest corner of the state, is suggestive of a relatively early push into the area by the big game hunters. That the hunters may have stayed for some time is indicated by data to be reviewed in following pages.

A gray chert specimen showing slight polish and incipient patination is in some ways one of the most intriguing fluted blades found in Michigan (Pl. IV, D). Although included in Table II data, it warrants detailed description. It was collected prior to 1928 in Washtenaw County by W. B. Hinsdale. More specific provenience information is not recorded, but the specimen is preserved in the Museum of Anthropology, Division of the Great Lakes.

Clearly, the point had been found by Archaic or Woodland peoples long after its original loss by the Early Man hunters, because it is modified for re-use by deep side-notching. In view of this reworking, the specimen was certainly not lost by Paleo-Indians at the locus of its discovery by Hinsdale. Except for side-notching, the projectile point is very much like a Folsom in outline, with the widest section at or just above the middle of the blade and with the sides almost parallel but tapering slightly from a maximum width of 18.0 mm. to a basal width of 14.5 mm. It is 42.5 mm. long and has a maximum thickness of 6.0 mm. The basal depth is 3.0 mm. Both faces are fluted, the length of fluting being 24.0 mm. and 11.5 mm., respectively, with single channel spalls removed in both cases. Above the fluting on both faces is a rudely defined median ridge. Lateral and basal grinding is heavy and is interrupted on the lateral edges by the later imposition of side-notching, the flake scars of which impinge on the flutes. Aside from notching, the artifact was not further subjected to modification by its later adaptive users. The side-notching was effected by percussion, with subsequent trimming not followed by grinding. Patination, but lightly developed, is somewhat more pronounced above the notched stemmed area.

Ottawa, Allegan, and Van Buren Counties

A fluted point found in Ottawa County in western Michigan is strictly limited in age by old lake levels. This specimen (see bottom of Table III) came from a sand blowout near the Pigeon River in the center of Section 3, Olive Township, at an elevation of between 610 and 620 feet above sea level (H. W. Moll, correspondence; and G. I. Quimby, verbal communication). Lake levels virtually precluded occupation of this locality until about 11,500 B. P. during the low-water stage correlative with the Two Creeks Interstadial. Much of the area was again inundated during Valders time, when the Calumet stage of Glacial Lake Chicago stood at 620 feet A. T. With the transition from the Calumet to the Toleston stage (605 feet) between 10,000 and 9,500 years ago, this section of Ottawa County was available for exploitation and has remained so through Lake Algonquin times on up to the present day.

According to Robert A. Hard, several other finds of fluted blades may have been made in Ottawa County along Crockery Creek, east of Grand Haven, but further information on these alleged finds is lacking.

A single fluted point from near South Haven, Van Buren County, and two from Lee Township, Allegan County, are probably limited in age by the same factors operating in Olive Township, Ottawa County. Elevational data are not available for these finds, but the superposition of their general provenience on the geological maps suggests that the finds must be post-Mankato in age. With the possible exception of the Valders Maximum, locational factors indicate that the artifacts could probably date during or any time after Two Creeks (compare distributional map with Maps 3 and 4).

Newaygo and Mecosta Counties

Two fluted points have been reported from the great sandy plain north of the Muskegon River in Newaygo County. George I. Quimby has confirmed the outwash nature of this plain (verbal communication), which may be correlated with the Lake Border morainic system (cf. Bretz, 1951a:426; Martin, 1955; and Map 2, herein). Since, as already noted, the Lake Border system is Late Cary in origin, the Newaygo artifacts cannot long antedate the Mankato Maximum, of about 12,500 years before the present, and may, theoretically, date any time thereafter within the time span of fluted-blade production. A speciman from northeastern and one from southeastern Mecosta County are subject to essentially the same limiting factors.

The extant ice fronts in Valders and Mankato times were in places not far removed from these loci. The northern areas of ice-free land were probably greatly subject to bog and marsh conditions. It seems most likely that the Newaygo and Mecosta fluted points date either during the Two Creeks Interstadial or sometime after the Valders Maximum, perhaps during Toleston or Lake Algonquin times (10,000 to 8,500 B. P). The latter interpretation is more consistent with the data from Bay and Wayne counties discussed below.

Bay and Wayne Counties

Although Bay and Wayne counties are some distance apart, they are considered together, since the fluted points found in both areas seem to reflect the same relative age. The Wayne County specimen, which is accompanied by site-specific provenience data, is from the northeastern corner of the county, close to the original shore line of Lake Algonquin in that area. Two from Bay County are from the west-central part of Frazer Township landward from the Algonquin beach (compare Map 1 with Map 5). These specimens could date from Two Creeks time, when lake levels were greatly reduced in all of the Great Lakes basins. If they are coeval with Lake Algonquin and thus date around 8,500 years ago, as determined by radiocarbon for the fully developed lake stage (Zumberge and Potzger, 1956:277, Fig. 4), it seems strange that other fluted points have not been found farther to the north. Aside from relatively minor flooding of what are now shore areas of Lake Huron, the Lower Peninsula was open to human exploitation in Lake Algonquin times, as far north as central Presque Isle and Cheboygan counties and southern Emmet County, and remained so through Nipissing times, but with even more land area uncovered in Lake Chippewa times. Subsequently, Michigan assumed its modern shore lines. North of Bay County, however, even more recent Indian sites are relatively scarce, possibly a result of ecological factors since the deciduous forests to the north are largely replaced by coniferous and mixed coniferous-deciduous communities (Hinsdale, 1932). Whether analogous conditions prevailed 8,500 years ago remains to be demonstrated by paleobotanists. On the basis of the limited evidence, it may be tentatively assumed that the fluted points of Wayne and Bay counties date around the time of either Lake Toleston or Lake Algonquin, or between 9,500 and 8,500 B. P., and probably not later.

Other Localities

Other finds of fluted points in Michigan are less directly susceptible to correlations suggested on geochronological bases. The two specimens from eastern Lapeer County, for instance, could date any time after the retreat of the Cary ice, as judged by the mapping of glacial lake shores in the eastern part of the Lower Peninsula.

The interesting cluster of fluted blades from several localities in Midland and Saginaw counties must certainly be later than the second attained stage of Lake Warren in the Huron Basin because of the high water plane expressed. These artifacts may also be later than lakes Grassmere-Lundy, but they may likewise date at any time thereafter during the Paleo-Indian Period. If these finds are contemporaries of the Bay County material, they should indicate the northernmost and latest occupational phase of the fluted-blade makers.

Remarks

Much of the foregoing has been necessarily tentative. Nevertheless, the suggested correlations seem reasonable in the light of present knowledge and are compatible with the time levels established and assumed for manifestations of Early Man in the High Plains and Southwest.

An antiquity for the Michigan fluted blades beginning about 13,500 years ago and ending, at the latest, by 8,500 years ago is suggested. The maximum date of 13,500 B. P. coincides nicely with the estimate of Greenman, Griffin, and Spaulding (1956:30) mentioned in the Introduction. If the temporal scale is substantiated by independent means (ideally by radiocarbon-dated material with definite cultural and, let us hope, faunal associations) one may anticipate that fluted-blade assemblages in other areas of the northeastern United States will prove to be of a comparable antiquity.

COMPARISONS AND DISCUSSION

The fluted points found in the Lower Peninsula of Michigan are but one manifestation of a widespread and probably gradual penetration of the Northeast by peoples of an Upper Paleolithic cultural stage who presumably subsisted by hunting. Such large Pleistocene animals as the mastodon may have furnished part of their food supply.[7] This quarry is inferred from kill sites of the fluted-blade hunters in the High Plains and Southwest but has yet to be directly established in the East by excavational data. It is probably only a matter of time before this will be done. On the basis of numerous finds, it seems likely that Paleo-Indians were in other areas of the northeastern United States at about the same time they were in Michigan. Relationships to this material are briefly explored below.

Comparative Material from Wisconsin

Douglas S. Byers, in 1942, briefly reported on two fluted blades found in Wisconsin. One of them is similar to specimens described from Michigan except that it is unusually crude. It was found near Royalton on the Waupaca River in Waupaca County. The other was found near the Yahara River on the west side of Lake Kegonsa, just south of Madison in Dane County, Wisconsin. It is diagnostically Folsom and shows the basal-nipple striking platform and the fine tangs characteristic of that type. It is fully fluted on both faces (Byers, 1942: 400, Fig. 2). George I. Quimby is making a study, as was mentioned above, of fluted-blade distributions in Wisconsin in the hope of correlating this information with Late Pleistocene features of time-index value. The results of his study will be of more than passing interest in view of suggestions made here. No "classic" Folsom points are as yet known from Michigan. If the locally discovered artifacts with which I

[7]Indications of Early Man in Michigan are not confined to fluted points but include several other forms of projectile points, the ramifications of which it has not been feasible to pursue in this monograph. Such other projectile points include Sandia-like single-shouldered blades; certain other forms which, if found in the West, would certainly be classified as Plainview, a seemingly locally specialized variant of the latter which is characteristically heavy, broad, and short for its size, and which always exhibits pronounced constriction above the basal ears (it is never fluted, although basally thinned, and is heavily ground along the edges); and some other points which strongly suggest Eden, Scottsbluff, Dalton or Meserve, Graham Cave Fluted, and Angostura. It is my impression that these early artifacts are particularly numerous in the southern part of the state. Additionally, there is an interesting manifestation of extremely hard argillite projectile points which recapitulate to a marked degree the over-all shape and even flaking pattern of Eden and, especially, Scottsbluff points. The associations of all of this material are as yet conjectural.

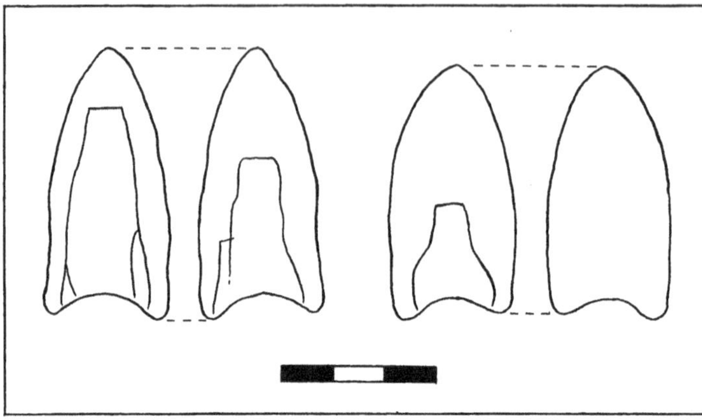

Fig. 3. Blade Configuration of Two Fluted Points from Waukesha County, Wisconsin.

have been dealing are equated with Clovis and if the temporal priority of Clovis over Folsom holds east of the Mississippi, wherever Folsom points are identified, this Wisconsin Folsom point may prove to belong near the upper limits of the Paleo-Indian Period as suggested for Michigan.

Also from Wisconsin are two interesting fluted points, heretofore unpublished, manufactured of Baraboo (?) quartzite. These specimens are in the collection of Professor Bennett Weaver, of the University of Michigan, who kindly brought them to the Museum of Anthropology for my inspection (Figure 3). Weaver found them close together one and a half miles south of Sussex, Lisbon Township, Waukesha County, Wisconsin (approximately 16 miles west-northwest of Milwaukee), on a knoll of Niagara dolomite. One of the specimens is fluted on both faces. It is 51.0 mm. long, has a maximum width of 23.0 mm. (at the base), and has a maximum thickness of 6.5 mm. near the tip. Basal depth is 4.0 mm., and the fluting scars are 34.0 and 30.0 mm. long, respectively. They bear evidence of the removal of subsidiary longitudinal flakes to widen the fluting. It is ground heavily on the base and laterally for 25.0 mm. up the edges on each side. The other specimen, also of what may be Baraboo quartzite, is 48.0 mm. long and 24.0 mm. wide (just below the middle of the blade), and is 22.0 mm. wide at the base. Its maximum thickness is 7.0 mm., and the basal depth is 3.5 mm. It too is ground basally, and lateral grinding extends for 20.0 mm. up the edges. It is fluted on one face only, and the scar is 18.0 mm. in length. Both of the points exhibit slight polish due to weathering.

The locus of the two fluted blades seems to lie between the Valparaiso and the Lake Border morainic systems (Alden, 1918: Pls. IV and XXIII). The artifacts cannot date, therefore, as early as the Valparaiso, but could date as early as about 14,000 years ago, when the Late Cary ice built the Lake Border moraine to the east of the find site. Furthermore, the maxima of the later Mankato and Valders did not glaciate the immediate area, and it was apparently never inundated by any of the glacial lake stages of the Lake Michigan Basin (Alden, 1918: Fig. 20). The specimens could date at any time later, of course, but their provenience and relationship to the Lake Michigan lobe moraines, coupled with an apparently early time horizon for fluted points in southwestern Michigan, suggests that an age of about 14,000-13,500 B. P. is likely.

Comparative Material from Ontario

Of crucial importance, likewise, are the ages of eastern Canadian fluted points. Kidd (1951:260) has illustrated eight from the province of Ontario which fall, with one possible exception, within the known configurational range of Michigan specimens. Concerning their distribution Kidd says that "such artifacts have been reported fairly widely distributed from the county of Elgin at the extreme southwestern limits of the Province to Lanark County in the east. The majority, however, have been found in the central and southwestern counties. The points in the Royal Ontario Museum of Archaeology which are not illustrated come respectively from Rideau Lake in Lanark County, Ameliasburg township, Prince Edward county, and from the shore of Rice Lake, Hamilton township, Northumberland county."

A thoroughly trustworthy estimate of the age of these specimens must await more intensive geochronological studies in southwestern and central Ontario.[8] I would hazard a guess, however, and place them at a time not much later than Lake Algonquin (9,000-8,000 B. P.). The four artifacts from Middlesex County, and one each from Elgin and Brant counties, may actually be pre-Valders or even pre-Mankato (but definitely post-Cary) in age (see Flint, 1953:268, Fig. 57). I would expect, in view of the limited distribution of Ontario fluted points, that their age would be found to be compatible with the Michigan chronology.

St. Louis Area of Missouri and Illinois

In comparing the Michigan collection with those from other eastern areas, one is faced with a relative dearth of consistently described materials. What description there is—and much of it is excellent—is

[8]Farther south, in New York State, William A. Ritchie has been making a somewhat similar study, of Paleo-Indian manifestations (Ritchie, 1957). I heard Ritchie's conclusions in a paper presented in New York City in December of 1956, before a meeting of Section H (Anthropology) of the American Association for the Advancement of Science. In that paper Ritchie proposed a much more recent age for fluted points in the New York State area than that entertained here. His chronological framework, based on present geological opinion in his area, is certainly too conservative, and is not consistent with the data from the rest of the Northeast and the Mississippi Valley.

scattered through professional and local journals. It is beyond the scope of this monograph to attempt a synthesis of the eastern data, but a few observations are offered as a framework for the better understanding of the Michigan series.

Michigan fluted points contrast in some particulars with those reported from within a hundred-mile radius of St. Louis in the central Mississippi Valley of southwestern Illinois and eastern Missouri (Smail, 1951). According to Smail, a large but unspecified number of fluted blades have been discovered in this area. Formwise, most of these points may be duplicated in the Lower Peninsula of Michigan, although the extremely long and narrow shape of what Smail calls "Ohio Fluted similarity" and the few exotic sports are unknown or unreported. Smail's published sample, which appears to be a representative one, exhibits an average length of 100.5 mm., within a range of 49.0 to 174.0 mm. for 27 unbroken measured artifacts; this length should be compared with the Michigan average of 53.0 mm., within a range of 21.0 to 120.0 mm. for 69 complete blades. Additional data on three other fluted points from Illinois fall within the St. Louis area range (Fowler, 1954, and Dan F. Morse, personal communication). This marked difference in average and range of blade length is all the more interesting in view of information from Ohio. Unfortunately, a usable body of data from other parts of Illinois and from Indiana is lacking.

Ohio-Pennsylvania Area

In 1936 Henry C. Shetrone published an article on fluted points from Ohio, in which he listed 140 specimens as stored in the Ohio State Museum. From a measured sample of 118 specimens a length range (transcribed from inches) of 33.0 to 140.0 mm. yielded an average of 79.0 mm. Blade configurations of the Ohio sample (Shetrone, 1936:249, Fig. 1) are again paralleled by many of those in Michigan, except that the fish-tailed variant, with marked constriction of the blade above the flaring basal ears, and the elongate, isosceles-triangle forms are lacking in the north. These particular forms, with a good deal of variation, have been called "Ohio Fluted" (see page 15). This unfortunate terminology is almost meaningless as a classificatory or even broadly descriptive designation. The forms which it seeks to embrace are as internally varied as are the forms it supposedly excludes, and so-called "Ohio Fluted" points are as characteristic of some parts of Tennessee, West Virginia, Virginia, Pennsylvania, New Jersey, and so forth, as they are of Ohio. A lot more descriptive and distributional material will be required before the taxonomists can really go to work on northeastern fluted points.

Concerning stone material, Shetrone (1936:255) points out the interesting fact that no Ohio fluted blades are manufactured of flint from the famous quarries at Flint Ridge. His observation may be extended to apply equally to Michigan and to western Pennsylvania, where Flint

Ridge material was used by many later peoples. In the latter region and in adjacent areas of Ohio, New York, West Virginia, and the western tip of Maryland, drained by the upper Ohio River, fluted blades have been reported which show specific resemblances to the Michigan artifacts in size, shape, and extent of fluting, and which are probably of comparable antiquity. Some of these have been fluted by the triple-channel flake technique (Mayer-Oakes, 1955:44), which is one of the characteristics of the Enterline Chert Industry in eastern Pennsylvania and possibly present as a minor trait in Michigan.

Eastern Pennsylvania, New Jersey, Delaware, and Virginia

The Enterline Industry, at least as represented at the Shoop site in southeastern Pennsylvania, is a remarkably uniform one which exhibits more restriction in size (length range is 38.0 to 60.0 mm.), blade configuration, and material than is usually true for other fluted-blade assemblages (Witthoft, 1952). Additionally, and in some contrast to the Michigan series, all of the Shoop points are fluted on both faces. These distinctions may not be quite as meaningful as they seem, since one is here comparing the finds from a single site (probably occupied over a relatively short time) with other finds from a state-wide survey.

Along the Atlantic littoral and, by extension, the piedmont areas descending to the coastal plain in eastern Pennsylvania, New Jersey, Delaware, and Virginia, numerous fluted points have been found. A greater employment of quartz and quartzite in the southern part of this area probably reflects differential availability of materials and not cultural selection. Information I have been collecting in the "Delaware Valley Fluted Point Survey" (Mason, 1957) may be compared with the Michigan data. Of 45 unbroken fluted points from this watershed, there are only a few specimens which cannot be directly matched, aside from material, with the Michigan artifacts. The Delaware Valley fluted blades have a length range of 25.0 to 102.0 mm., with an average of 55.0 mm. All Michigan forms are recapitulated in this region, but not all Delaware Valley forms are represented in Michigan. There is, for instance, a usually large and bilaterally symmetrical ovoid blade which is not found in Michigan. The differences observed between these two areas are of a nature to be expected where local resources vary and where spatial and, perhaps, also temporal factors intervene.

The Williamson site in Dinwiddie County, Virginia, has been suggested by Witthoft (1952:486), as representing a southern extension of the Enterline Industry, partly because of the use of certain eastern Pennsylvania jaspers found on the site. Whether the relationship between Williamson and Shoop is as close as Witthoft seems to think is a question not directly pertinent to this study. It is still of interest to note, however, that the lithic base of the Shoop artifacts is predominantly Onondaga chert and not Pennsylvania jaspers. Likewise, the Enterline Industry remains virtually unidentified in the neighboring

Delaware Valley, with the possible exception of two or three triple channel fluted projectile points, and one of the major sources of the Pennsylvania jaspers is, in fact, the Delaware drainage area. On the basis of this evidence and the typology, I suspect that the highly specialized Enterline Chert Industry is more geographically restricted than Witthoft suggests. The Delaware Valley and some of the Williamson specimens are very similar to those from the Lower Peninsula of Michigan; the Enterline points, however, are highly distinctive and could not be lost in a collection from any of these areas except, perhaps, a selected sample from the Williamson site itself.

Of the 30 measurable fluted points recovered at the Williamson site, an average length of 54.0 mm. has been determined within a range of from 26.0 to about 120.0 mm. (McCary, 1951:16). These artifacts differ from the Michigan series in having a high frequency of blades that are slightly constricted between the middle of the blade and the base, with distinct ears resulting. Broad pentagonal forms with extremely shallow bases are prominent features of the Williamson assemblage and occur also at the Reagen site in Vermont (Ritchie, 1953). They are absent in Michigan and apparently also at the Shoop site. Basal and lateral grinding is not as characteristic of the Virginia artifacts, being present on 21 out of 33 specimens (McCary, 1951:13), as it is of the Michigan series. As was noted for the Delaware Valley, the employment of quartz and quartzite for the fashioning of points in Virginia does not carry into Michigan, although it appears in Wisconsin.

New England Fluted Points

Among the closest northeastern resemblances to Michigan fluted points are those manifested at the Bull Brook site, in Ipswich, Massachusetts (Byers, 1954, 1955, and 1957). The involved specimens could easily be lost in a collection from Michigan, except that quasi-triangular forms are more prominent at Bull Brook (see Byers, 1954:346, Fig. 91). Length and width characteristics are included in the statement that the Bull Brook points are "remarkably uniform in size, ranging from 68-49 mm. in length, by 25-21 mm. in width" (Byers, 1954:345). The investigator of this important site recently estimated its age to be between 8,000 and 12,000 B. P. (Byers, 1957:51). The age of the Bull Brook manifestations however, may perhaps be estimated with more precision than Byers indicates, as a result of the radiocarbon data from Athol, Massachusetts, which seemingly date the Valders Maximum in that area. A date of 10,700 ± 800 years B. P. was determined for a wood sample 235 cm. below the surface of an old bog at Athol (M-413). The U. S. Geological Survey laboratory date (10,800) for the same sample was within a hundred years of the above. Griffin (1956, p. 21) states that "It can also be said that the situation of the Bull Brook site northeast of Boston, with its fluted blade assemblage (Byers, 1954), is in accord with the hypothesis that it is the earliest evidence of man in New England

and was occupied shortly after the glacial retreat." The radiocarbon data and their evaluation suggests a probable date of shortly after 10,700 B. P. for Bull Brook. This is compatible with information from the Lower Michigan Peninsula and supports the typological resemblances proposed here. The close relationship that Byers implies between the Bull Brook and Shoop sites seems open to question (compare plates and figures in Byers, 1954, with those in Witthoft, 1952).

The assemblage of fluted points at the Reagen site, northwestern Vermont, resembles in certain particulars, as the pentagonal blades, the Williamson complex, but it can only be remotely affiliated with the one from that station or from such others as Bull Brook, Shoop, and the fluted-blade series from Michigan. As suggested by Ritchie (1953:256), the Reagen artifacts probably belong to a late phase of the Paleo-Indian Period; they incorporate, for instance, incipient Archaic traits, including talc ornaments not otherwise known from eastern Early Man sites. The suggested age of this peculiar complex is sometime prior to 6,000 B. P. (Ritchie, 1953:257).

SUMMARY AND CONCLUSIONS

Of the fluted point assemblanges reviewed, I suggest that the Bull Brook artifacts most closely resemble, at least in terms of blade configuration, the specimens from the Lower Peninsula of Michigan. The Delaware Valley material, likewise, seems closely related. Fewer similarities are observed with the Williamson complex in Virginia, and the Shoop and Reagen sites offer the least comparable material. There is more variability in the Ohio and Illinois-Missouri artifacts than is expressed in the Michigan sample. This may indicate a local fluted-blade developmental area in the central Mississippi Valley where such points, on geological grounds, could be older than the Michigan specimens.

Although a satisfactory body of data on fluted-point characteristics is not yet available for Illinois (beyond the St. Louis area) and Indiana, this brief examination of Paleo-Indian finds in the Northeast indicates something else of interest. Northward and eastward from the St. Louis area fluted blades tend to become progressively smaller, not only in average size but in their minimum-maximum length range. Thus, the size of Ohio points is midway between the range and average noted for those of the St. Louis area and the Lower Michigan Peninsula, and, likewise, between those of the St. Louis area and stations on the East Coast. The implications of this interesting size shift, which is accompanied by retention of essentially similar blade shapes, cannot be further explored until more information is available from these and other areas.

I have noted that Michigan fluted points are typologically related to many others from the northeastern United States and Canada, and also to some of the projectile points of the big game hunters of the High Plains as exemplified by Folsom and, especially, by Clovis. Although still lacking associated faunal remains, if the Michigan series equates with Clovis, we are obliged to view them as a Great Lakes manifestation of the widespread Llano Complex defined by Sellards (1952:17-46), and to infer that the people who used such weapons were likewise hunters of such Pleistocene mammals as the American probiscideans.[9] Quimby's term "paleoeastern culture" is excellent since it recognizes the essential relatedness of the Plains and Eastern fluted blades (1954:317).

Fluted points are not a trait of the eastern Archaic cultures, but clearly belong to an early cultural horizon which had ceased to exist by the time of the development of the recognized Archaic manifestations. The Archaic began in the East between 8,000 and 9,000 years ago, as indicated by radiocarbon, and this is an antiquity comparable to that of the Plano Culture in the West (Eden, Scottsbluff, and others), which seems to have succeeded the fluted-blade peoples through what may be a transitional form in Plainview. It has been noted that Plainview-like projectile points have been found in Michigan. The idea that fluted projectile points were a vestigial trait carried up into relatively late times in

[9]For an excellent and concise summary of the associations of extinct fauna with particular projectile point types in the western United States, see Jelinek, 1957.

the East after their disappearance in the Plains, is unsupported by the evidence from Michigan.[10]

Typological considerations seem to be supported by the geochronological evidence in Michigan. An age of 13,500 B. P. for the earliest appearance of man in the state is suggested by this evidence, and a date for the close of the fluted-blade complex in this region of around 8,500 B. P. appears indicated. It is shown that Paleo-Indians apparently began moving into Michigan from the south (probably the southwest) following closely on the retreating margins of the Cary ice. A uniform and slowly changing hunting culture is inferred from the scattered remains. Unless new geochronological discoveries or radiocarbon age determinations radically affect the scheme upon which these dates are based, it is felt that this study will demonstrate that concepts of a Paleo-Indian priority in the West are not as well founded as they may once have seemed. An antiquity for the eastern Paleo-Indian Period, at least as expressed in the Upper Great Lakes area, approximately equal to that of the Plains and Southwest is certainly indicated, if not proved.

---

[10]The fact that a few fluted points have been found on eastern Archaic sites is irrelevant. They have also been found in the fill of Ohio Hopewell mounds.

LITERATURE CITED

Alden, William C.

1918 The Quaternary Geology of Southeastern Wisconsin. U. S. Geol. Surv., Prof. Paper 106. Washington, D. C.

Antevs, Ernst

1953 Geochronology of the Deglacial and Neothermal Ages. Journ. Geol., 61:195-230.

1954 Geochronology of the Deglacial and Neothermal Ages: a Reply. *Ibid.*, 62:516-20.

1955 Varve and Radiocarbon Chronologies Appraised by Pollen Data. *Ibid.*, 63:495-99.

1957 Geological Tests of the Varve and Radiocarbon Chronologies. *Ibid.*, 65:129-48.

Bretz, J. Harlen

1951a The Stages of Lake Chicago: Their Causes and Correlations. Amer. Journ. Sci., 249: 401-29.

1951b Causes of the Glacial Lake Stages in Saginaw Basin, Michigan. Journ. Geol., 59:244-58.

Byers, Douglas S.

1942 Fluted Points from Wisconsin. Amer. Antiq., 7, No. 4:400.

1954 Bull Brook—A Fluted Point Site in Ipswich, Massachusetts. *Ibid.*, 19, No. 4:343-51.

1955 Additional Information on the Bull Brook Site, Massachusetts. *Ibid.*, 20, No. 3:274-76.

1957 Ipswich B. C. Bull. Mass. Archaeol. Soc., 18, No. 3:49-55.

Crane, H. Richard

1956 University of Michigan Radiocarbon Dates I. Science, 124:664-72.

Flint, Richard Foster

1953 Glacial Geology and the Pleistocene Epoch. Fourth Printing. New York: John Wiley and Sons.

1956 New Radiocarbon Dates and Late-Pleistocene Stratigraphy. Amer. Journ. Sci., 254:265-87.

1957 Glacial and Pleistocene Geology. New York: John Wiley and Sons.

Fowler, Melvin L.

1954 Some Fluted Projectile Points from Illinois. Amer. Antiq., 20, No. 2:170-71.

Green, Amos R.

MS Early Man and His Descendents in Berrien County. Unpublished manuscript.

Greenman, Emerson F., James B. Griffin, and Albert C. Spaulding

1956 Notes on the Prehistory of the Upper Great Lakes Area. Friends of the Pleistocene Guidebook, Midwest Sect., pp. 30-33. Ann Arbor. (Mimeographed.)

Griffin, James B.
1956 The Reliability of Radiocarbon Dates for Late Glacial and Recent Times in Central and Eastern North America. Anthropological Papers, Dept. Anthropol., Univ. Utah, No. 26 (papers of the Third Great Basin Archeological Conference), edited by Robert Anderson, pp. 10-34. Salt Lake City.

Hinsdale, W. B.
1932 Distribution of the Aboriginal Population of Michigan. Occ. Contrib. Mus. Anthropol. Univ. Mich., No. 2.

Hough, Jack L.
1953 Pleistocene Chronology of the Great Lakes Region. Mimeographed report, University of Illinois and the Office of Naval Research, Contract No. NGORI-07133, Project NR-018-122. Urbana.
1956 The Great Lakes from the Glenwood and Warren Stages to the Algonquin Stage. Friends of the Pleistocene Guidebook, Midwest Sect., p. 20. Ann Arbor. (Mimeographed.)

Jelinek, Arthur J.
1957 Pleistocene Faunas and Early Man. Papers Mich. Acad. Science, Arts, and Letters, 43:225-37.

Kidd, Kenneth E.
1951 Fluted Points in Ontario. Amer. Antiq., 16, No. 3:260.

Krieger, Alex D.
1947 Certain Projectile Points of the Early American Hunters. Bull. Texas Archaeol. and Paleontol. Soc., 18:7-27.

Leighton, M. M.
1933 The Naming of the Sub-Divisions of the Wisconsin Glacial Age. Science, N. S., 77:168.
1957 The Cary-Mankato-Valders Problem. Journ. Geol., 65, No. 1:108-11.

Leighton, M. M., and H. E. Wright, Jr.
1957 Radiocarbon Dates of Mankato Drift in Minnesota. Science, 125: 1037-39.

Leverett, Frank, and F. B. Taylor
1915 The Pleistocene of Indiana and Michigan and the History of the Great Lakes. U. S. Geol. Surv., Monograph 53, Washington, D. C.

Martin, Helen M.
1955 Map of the Surface Formations of the Southern Peninsula of Michigan. Dept. Conserv., Geol. Surv. Div., Publ. 49.

Mason, Ronald J.
1957 Additional Fluted Point Data from Southeastern Pennsylvania. Penn. Archaeologist, 27, No. 1:39-42.

Mayer-Oakes, William J.
1955 Prehistory of the Upper Ohio Valley; An Introductory Archeological Study. Ann. Carnegie Mus., Vol. 34, Ser., No. 2. Pittsburgh.

McCary, Ben C.
1951 A Workshop Site of Early Man in Dinwiddie County, Virginia. Amer. Antiq., 17, No. 1:9-17.

Melhorn, W. N.
1954 Valders Glaciation of the Southern Peninsula of Michigan. Unpublished doctoral thesis, Univ. Mich.

Quimby, George I.
1954 Cultural and Natural Areas before Kroeber. Amer. Antiq., 19, No. 4: 317-31.
1958 Fluted Points and Geochronology of the Lake Michigan Basin. *Ibid.*, 23, No. 3, pp. 247-54. Salt Lake City.

Ritchie, William A.
1953 A Probable Paleo-Indian Site in Vermont. Amer. Antiq., 18, No. 3: 249-58.
1957 Traces of Early Man in the Northeast. New York State Mus. Sci. Serv. Bull. No. 358. Albany: Univ. State of New York.

Sellards, E. H.
1952 Early Man in America. Texas Mem. Mus. Publ. Austin.

Shetrone, Henry C.
1936 The Folsom Phenomenon as Seen from Ohio. Ohio State Archaeol. and Hist. Quart., 45, No. 3:240-256.

Smail, William
1951 Some Early Projectile Points from the St. Louis Area. Illinois State Archaeol. Soc., N. S., 2, No. 1:11-16.

Spurr, Stephen H., and James H. Zumberge
1956 Late Pleistocene Features of Cheboygan and Emmet Counties, Michigan. Amer. Journ. Sci., 254:96-109.

Williams, Stephen
1957 The Island 35 Mastodon: Its Bearing on the Age of Archaic Cultures in the East. Amer. Antiq., 22, No. 4, Pt. 1:359-72.

Witthoft, John
1952 A Paleo-Indian Site in Eastern Pennsylvania: An Early Hunting Culture. Proc. Amer. Philos. Soc., 96, No. 4:464-95.

Wormington, H. M.
1949 Ancient Man in North America. 3d.ed.; Denver: Denver Mus. Nat. Hist.

Zumberge, James H.
1956 Late Pleistocene History of the Lake Michigan Basin. Friends of the Pleistocene Guidebook, Midwest Sect., pp. 3-12. Ann Arbor. (Mimeographed.)

Zumberge, James H., and John E. Potzger
1955 Pollen Profiles, Radiocarbon Dating, and Geologic Chronology of the Lake Michigan Basin. Science, 121:309-11.
1956 Late Wisconsin Chronology of the Lake Michigan Basin Correlated with Pollen Studies. Geol. Soc. Amer. Bull., 67:271-88.

PLATES

PLATE I

Fluted Points from Michigan

A. Chert, Saginaw County.

B. White flint, county and site unknown.

C. Chert, Lapeer County.

D. Chert, Salem Township, Washtenaw County.

All of the specimens are in the collections of the Museum of Anthropology, University of Michigan.

Scale: approximately full size.

PLATE I

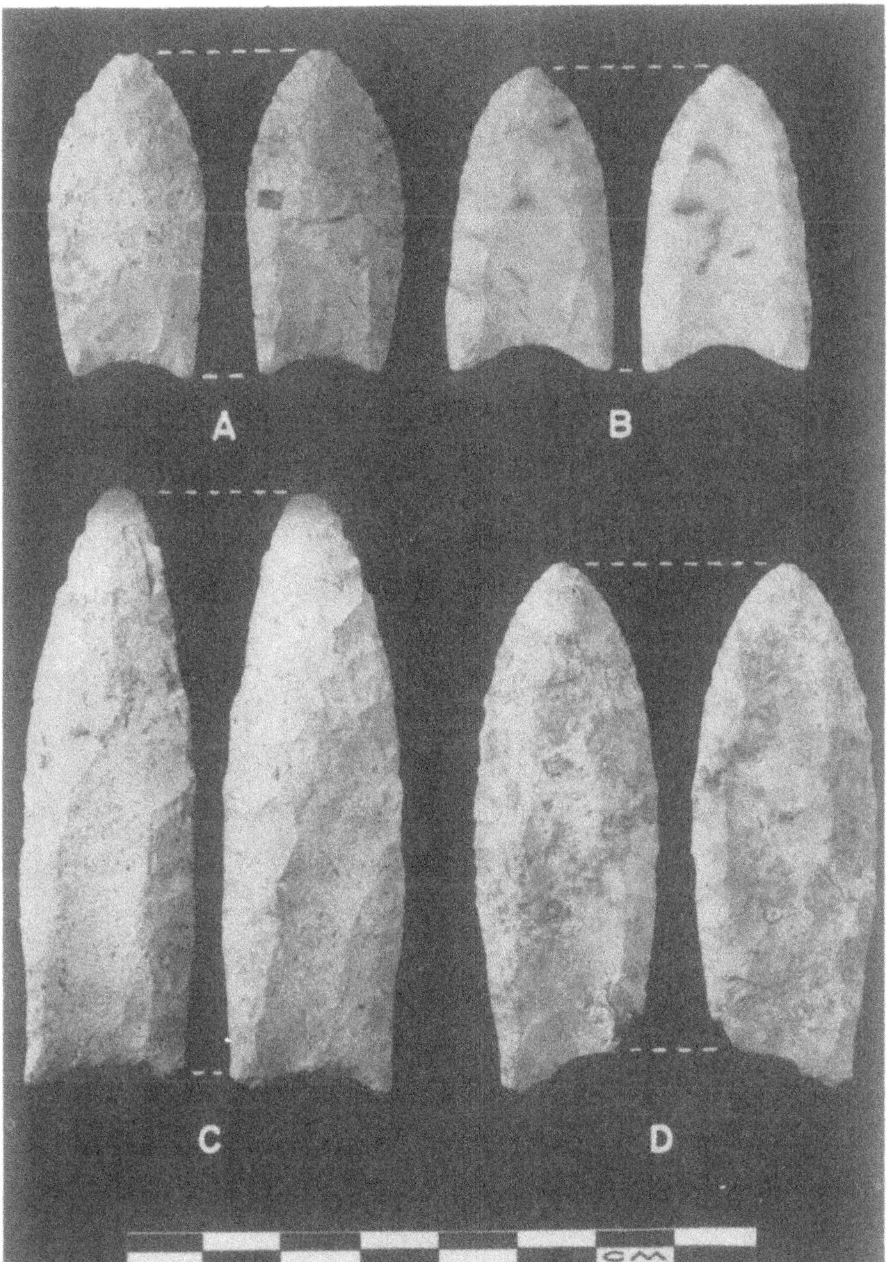

PLATE II

Fluted Points from Michigan

A. Chert, Lapeer County; note differential negative bulbar expression in the flutes, see pages 14 and 15.

B. Chert, Lapeer County.

C. Greenish chert, county and site unknown.

D. Flint, variegated; Washtenaw County.

All of the specimens are in the collections of the Museum of Anthropology, University of Michigan.

Scale: approximately full size.

PLATE II

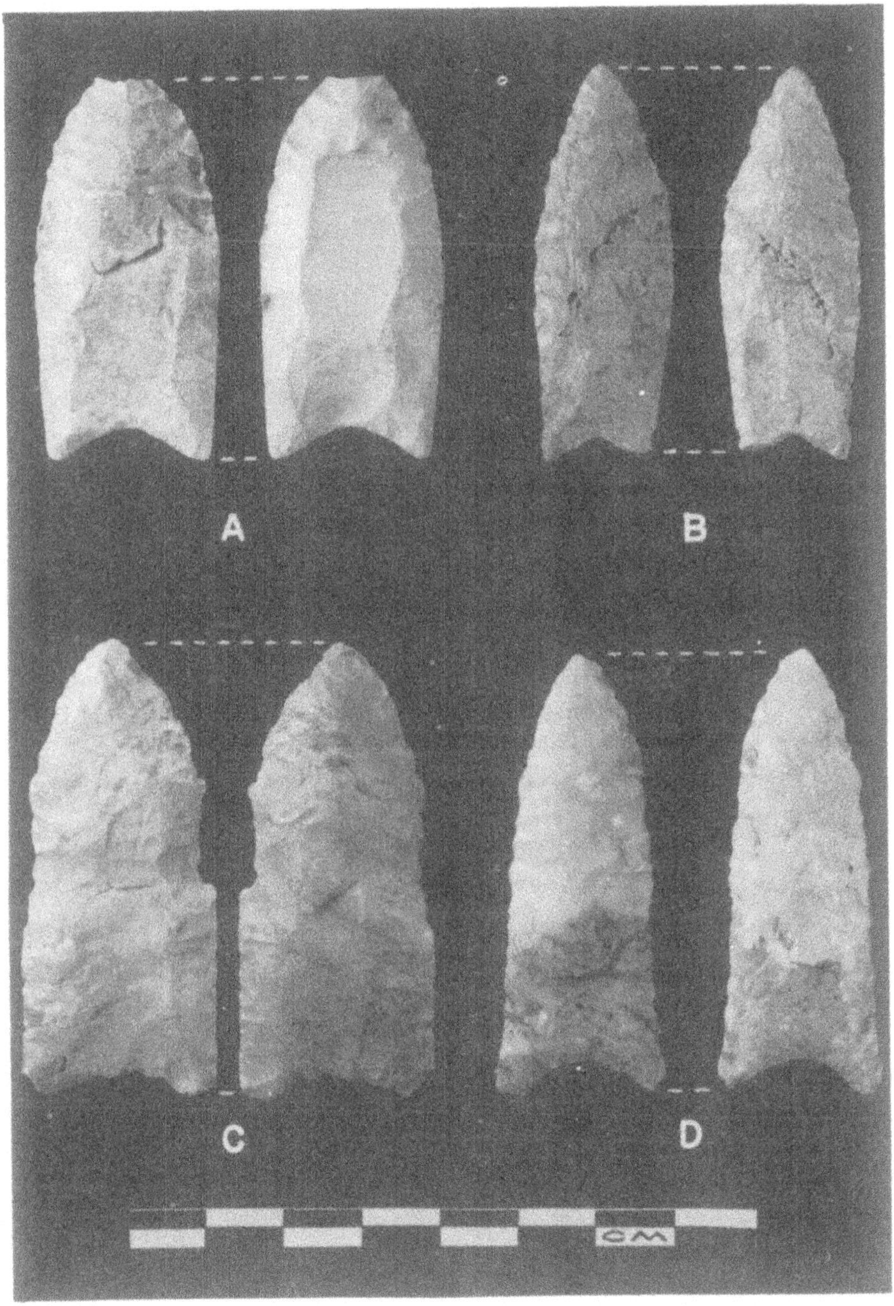

PLATE III

Fluted Points from Michigan

A. Variegated flint, Washtenaw County.

B. Chert, Hillsdale County.

C. Chalcedony, Lapeer County, see page 7.

All of the specimens are in the collections of the Museum of Anthropology, University of Michigan.

Scale: approximately full size.

PLATE III

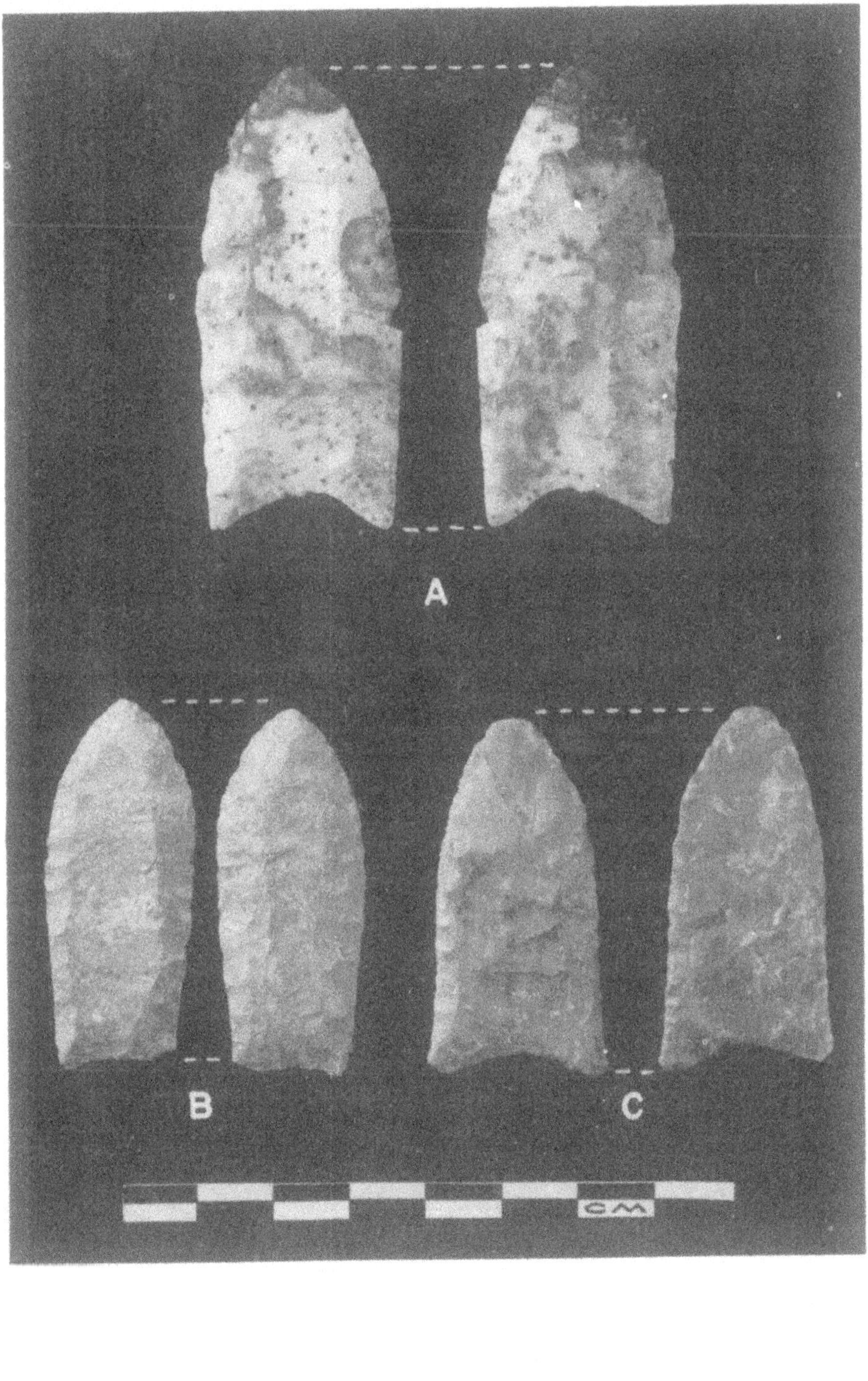

PLATE IV

Fluted Points from Michigan

A. Chert, Ann Arbor Township, Washtenaw County; an example of fluted-like, or quasi-fluted, points with the shape, grinding, and the like of fluted blades.

B. Chert, Ionia County; probably reworked from an originally longer blade.

C. Chert, county and site unknown.

D. Chert, Washtenaw County; example of a fluted point reworked by later peoples, see page 33.

All of the specimens are in the collections of the Museum of Anthropology, University of Michigan.

Scale: approximately full size.

PLATE IV

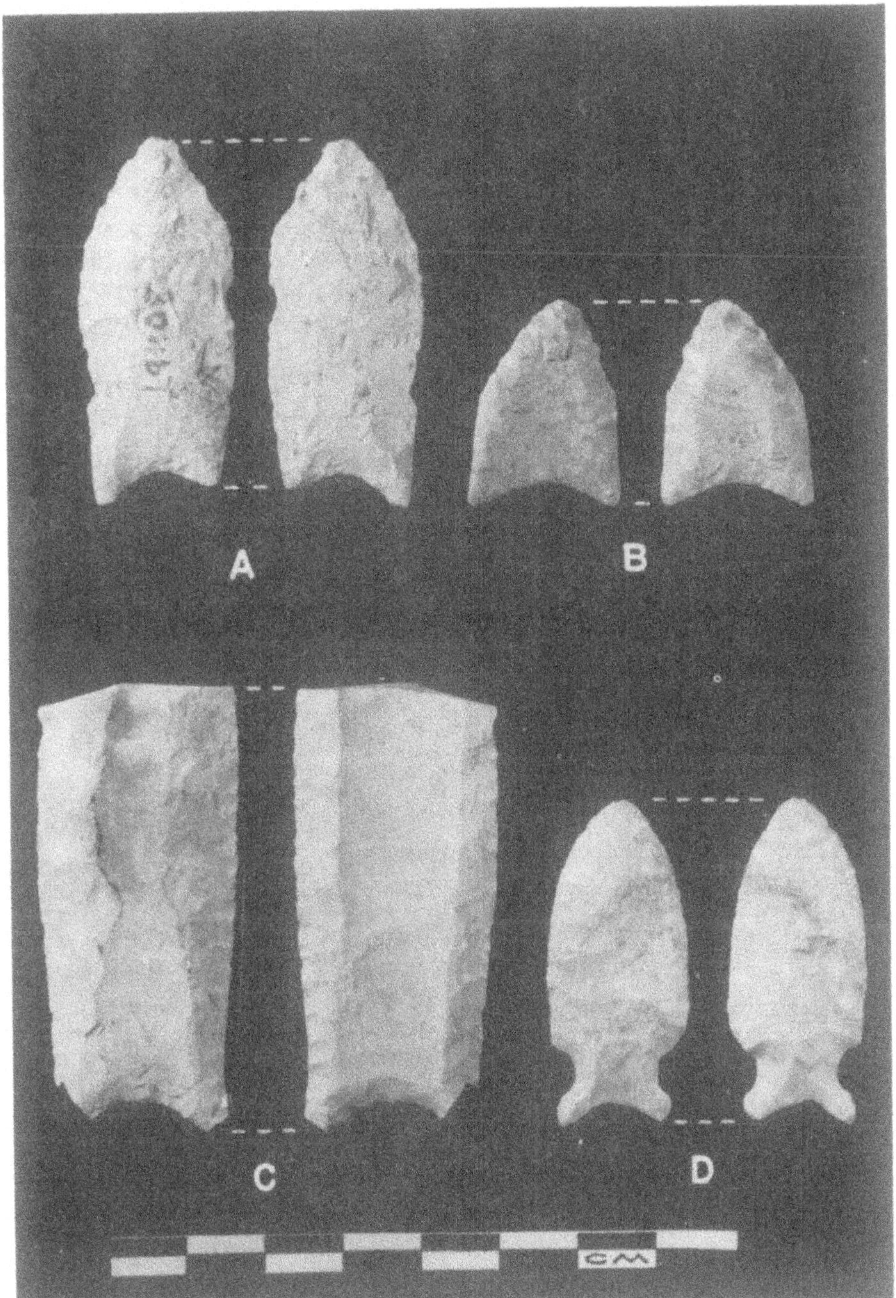

PLATE V

Fluted Blade from Michigan

Bifacially fluted flint blade secondarily used as a knife, Lodi Township, Washtenaw County. Longest edge bears characteristic features of tool use, the broken tip being a result of a blow struck near the tip.

The specimen is in the collections of the Museum of Anthropology, University of Michigan.

Scale: approximately full size.

PLATE V

PLATE VI

Fluted Points from Michigan

A. Chert, Washtenaw County.

B. Jasper, Washtenaw County.

The specimens are in the collections of the Museum of Anthropology, University of Michigan.

Scale: approximately full size.

PLATE VI

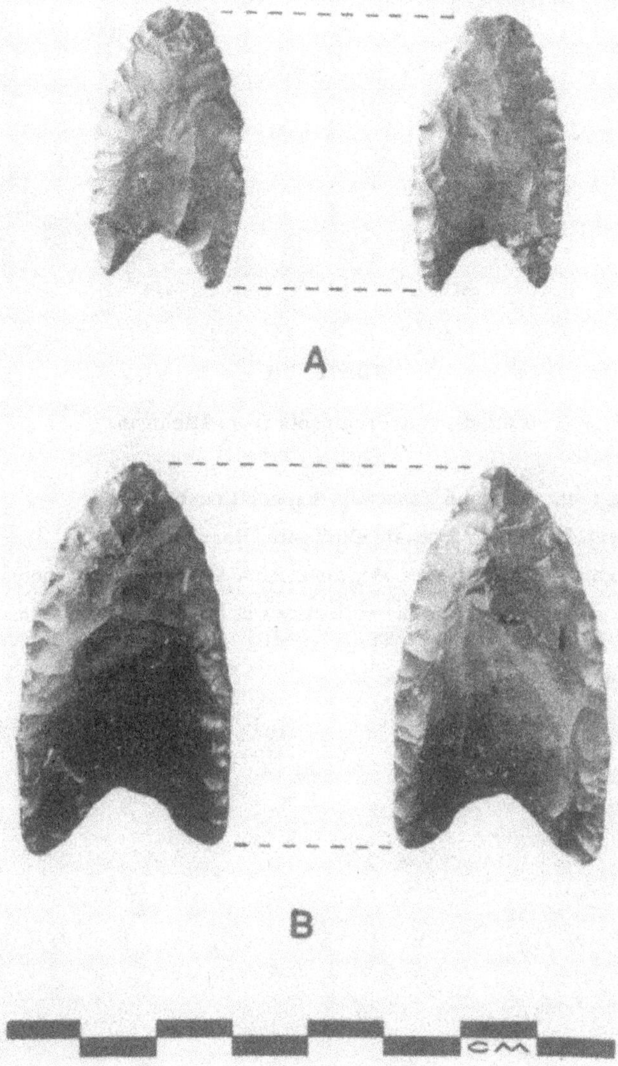

PLATE VII

Fluted-point Fragments from Michigan

A. Chert, from Goodland Township, Lapeer County.

B-C. Chert, from the Moccasin Bluff site, Berrien County.

D. Variegated flint, from the Moccasin Bluff site, Berrien County.

All of the specimens are in the collections of the Museum of Anthropology, University of Michigan, see page 32.

Scale: approximately full size.

PLATE VII

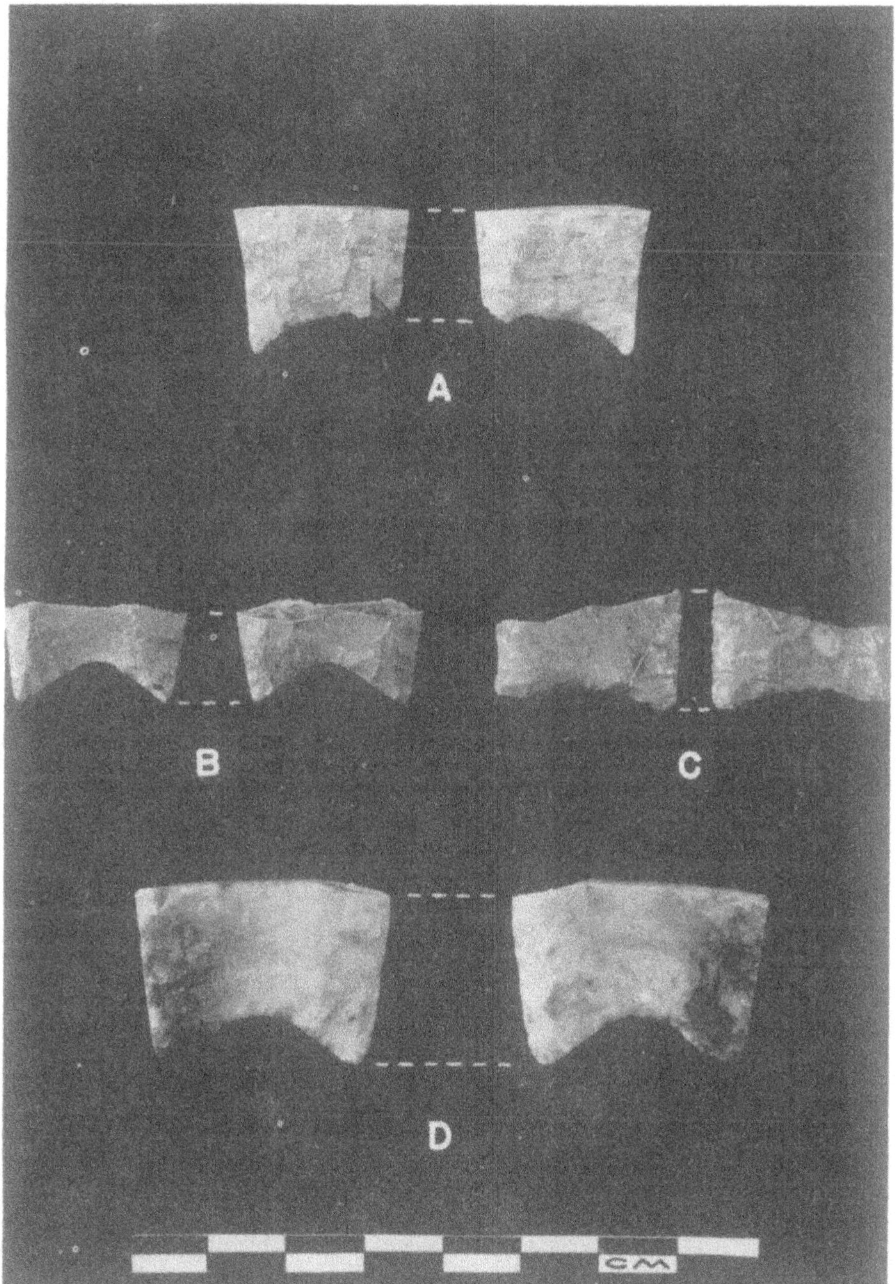

PLATE VIII

Fluted Points from Michigan

A. Chert, Lee Township, Allegan County. In the Paul Armintrout Collection.

B. Chert, Lee Township, Allegan County. In the Paul Armintrout Collection.

C. Chert, Berrien County. In the Amos R. Green Collection.

Scale: approximately full size.

PLATE VIII

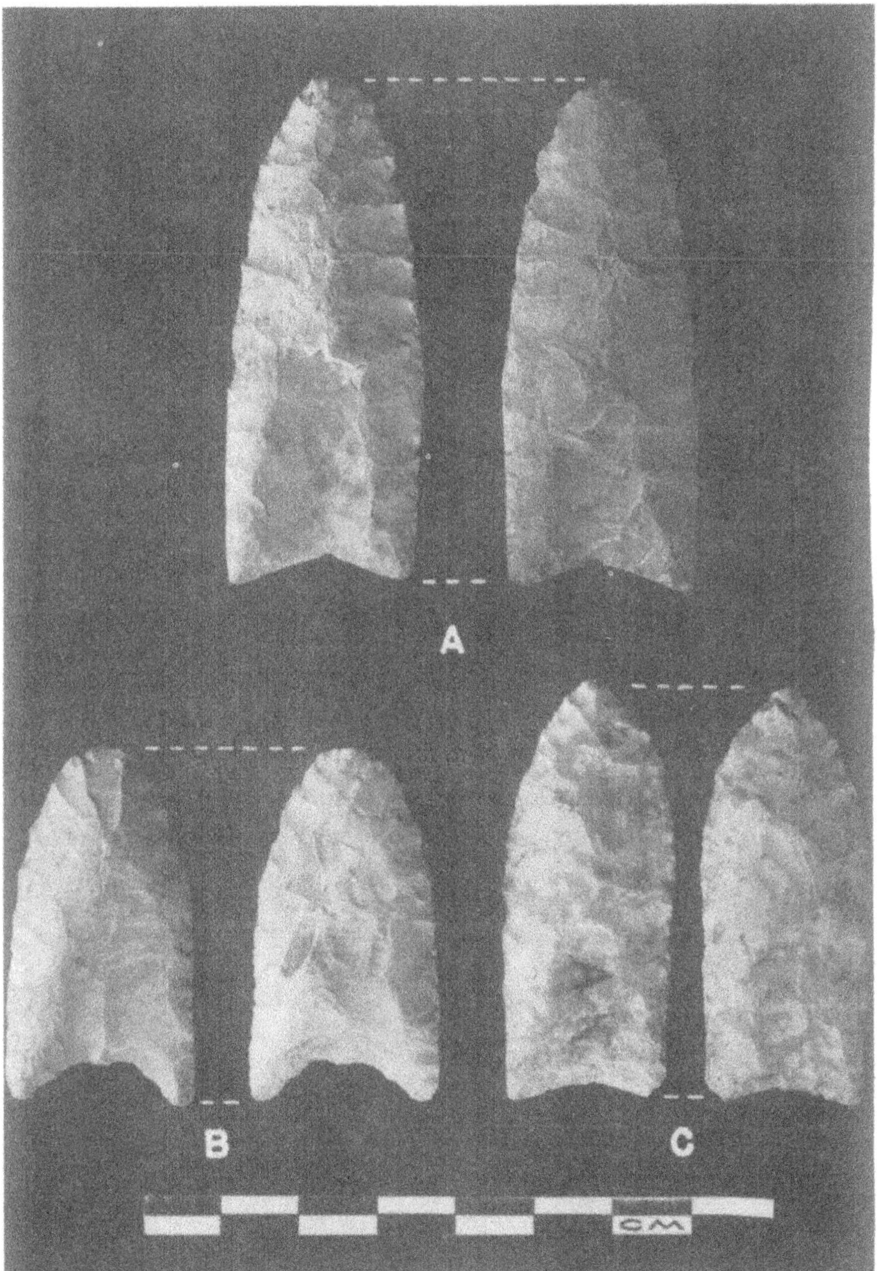

PLATE IX

Fluted Points from Michigan

A. Chert, St. Joseph County. In the Guy Nelson Collection.

B. Chert, Berrien County. In the Amos R. Green Collection.

C. Chert, Van Buren County. In the Guy Nelson Collection.

Scale: approximately full size.

PLATE IX

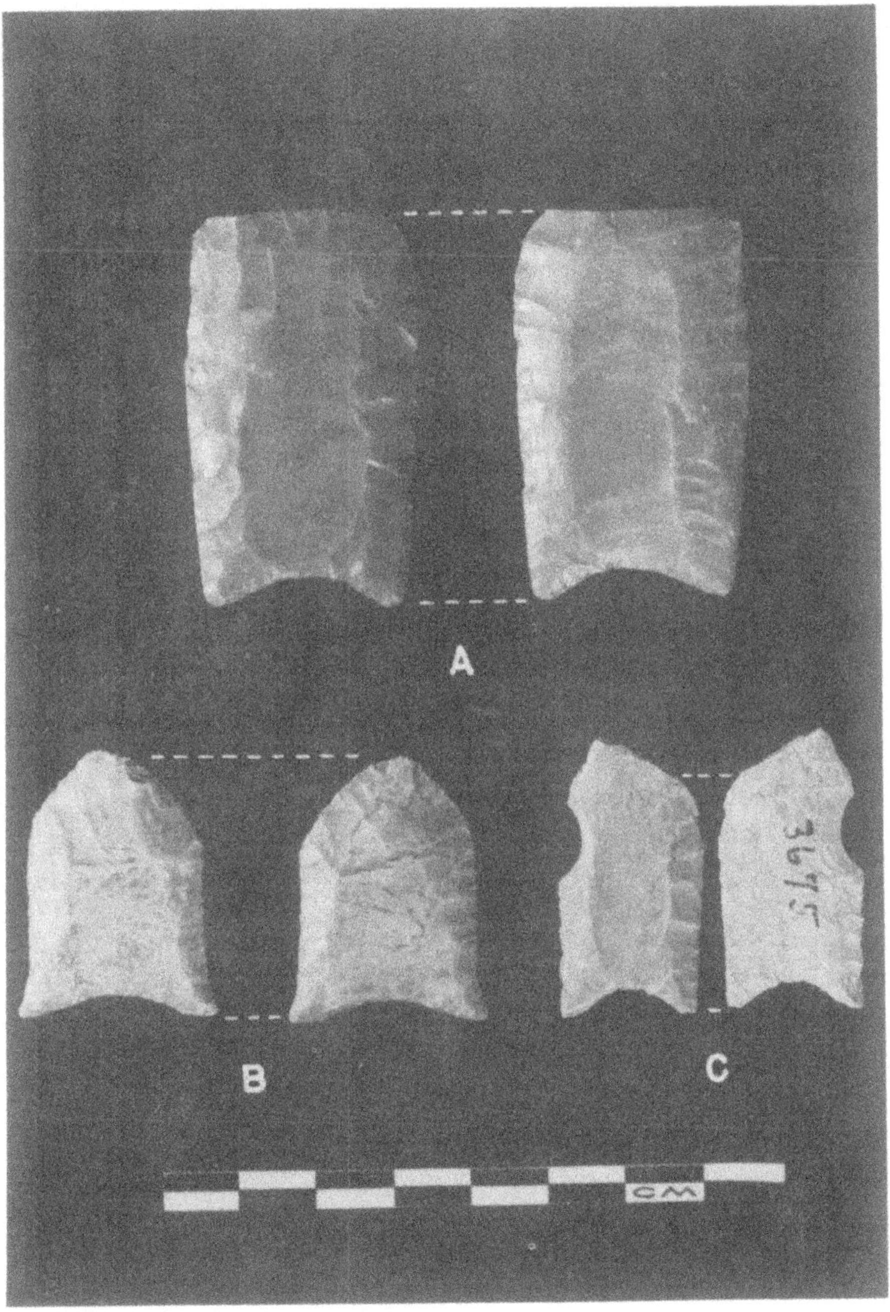

www.ingramcontent.com/pod-product-compliance
Lightning Source LLC
LaVergne TN
LVHW050022250826
846302LV00008B/65
* 9 7 8 1 9 4 9 0 9 8 3 2 7 *